# THE BLUE HORSE
# WIND

# THE BLUE HORSE WIND

Poems 2002-2012

## Anastacia Burns

River Sanctuary
PUBLISHING

*The Blue Horse Wind*
Copyright © 2012 by Anastacia Burns

Cover and interior design by River Sanctuary Graphic Arts

ISBN 978-1-935914-23-5

Printed in the United States of America

RIVER SANCTUARY PUBLISHING
P.O Box 1561
Felton, CA 95018
www.riversanctuarypublishing.com
*Dedicated to the awakening of the New Earth*

To Wes, Marlon, Daynan, Mariah
and Starlar

and to my mentor
Stan Rice

# CONTENTS

## I

## II

## III

# I

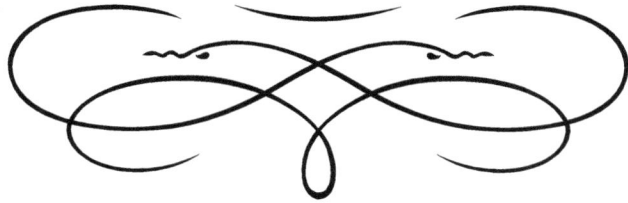

# THE EYELESS BLUE HORSE WIND

After the eyeless
blue horse wind
grew blades,
sprouting in rustling leaf waves
die hard
Nepenthe twilight
glittering unfurling
symphony in
blues layered
arpeggio skyscraping wings.
And
Learned to hear
through conch shell
 echoing ears,
the free dimensional
angels of angles,
the rapid pulsing vision in things;
galloping blindly
leaping over twisted
black weeping roots,
mute hooves
uprooting the toes
of nefarious imp
twirling parasols;
gill swelling
spongy umbrous fungus
coolie hatted mushrooms,
peasant loaned the loam
to nursery spread
the scion bred
leporous curse culture
of spores poring green fumes.

Until at last
the pulpy rising sporous nation,
methodized faceless mushy helmeted army

pushing, springing for world domination,
loosening, losing their springy toe
marching foot hold,
spuming fistfuls of fuming green
cursed
mummy dust powder,
TwinTower
collapsing
the wicked spell
syphliptic slut poisoning
the starry glass glinting
hushed
village of the damned.

2
Fugitive
flash backs
revolted,
slave breaking chains.
The nightmare nightshade
tugged open,
(for good karma
to natural mossy mocassin backtrack)
evanishing banishing
the sullen green faced vapors.
Thus
by inhaling
the fresh heavenly rush
aroused by the Pegasus crepuscular finger tipped wings,
and sensing the echoing revision
of the high spirited cerulean horse

the beware bogey Golem eyed
gypsy tattered ragbag
children,
riding unbridled green flaming nostril
midnight groomed night mares,
Mephistopheles disguised phantoms
rising from the hollow toothless pit

of the finger crossing witch's tree,
like flashing black lightening
unhitched,
tempest transported
from the thundering triton struck skeleton dust past

of the misery toe tagged
smouldering foot dragging
ash splashed
humble hunched orphans,
unreined by the skull and crossbone
mould face engraved
on their gangrene green, splotched blotched
moldering into a sunken mush,
doomed pumpkin homes.
Victims of the hoarse baying wind
cruelly lashed,
slashed
by the desperado exiled boneless shade
whose star bone spurs
spurred the blue bearded eyeless horse
to such barberous velocity
ferocity,
its teeth bit off
the gulping
altitude
of hissing
candle
wicks
dripping ash,
looting booting out
the last arch
of footless light.

But reined, saddled by the contagious plague
of decay,
Rifled
to perform shamefaced acts,
exposed to the bone

before the flesh stripped
wing polished ivory halls,
king-
dom
of the death courting prime evil spade face vultures.


3
The pale green jade-
ed
nagged by the precious stone-d
religious
reminisce
of their star crossed, once blooms day blooming
ripe agog foxfire tongued river
licking lapping at the wind horses'
bulging blue thighs,
whilst the equinus
lowered its cygnet neck,
muzzleless
swilling
guzzling
until drunk,
filling its bodiless body
with a deluge of swirling cumulus clouds;
the visionary water winged Pegasus
be-
hoof
pleased,
tease breeze levitating
over the fluid carnival mirror.


These cracked shell tree felled
un nested orphans,
further egg hatching
memoirs
of the umbilicus vine attached
nursery rhyming
everlasting gourd dome homes
they had in blithesome heights belonged to.

The poppy orange
of witch bewitched
flashed liquid foxfire
beneath
the engorged
Mars roaring
arterial flooding
fierce
carnivale orange
satyr horned
colossal gord
headless horseman
rapacious moon;
soon to release
from ogerous pitted
unlidded eyes,
a swarming orgy
of Morpheus charged electric rubric bees
stinging the setting sleepers
with chimeric dreams.

This curled antenna
fairy tail
silver thread
trimmed
skirt fringed rim,
lambs' wool closely knit
moonwort ferned
Cancer moonchild
ancient secret sylvan,
where they were moon spoon fed
by a blue mothman kinetic tribe
where
all were
one
and won.
Sublime
At eventide, surrounded by lime will o the wisp mist
drifting lifting from the nearby Marsh

King,
graceful
transcedental indigo caped
leaping silver fish
rapier beaked
meditating
on one stiff stilt leg,
keen green eyed
silvery feathered crane.


4
In spite of this grievous loss,
 it was not the venemous
spiked needle of vengence,
that needled them
to dare
creep into the unsealed hymen
entrance
glowing hellish red
in the jagged peak primitive distance.
Not the deep spade dug grave
of the broken hands
shattered clock
burials,
fated from the shrunken head
withered too late harvest
that even starved
their already skinny shadows
convinced to
stick somewhere beneath
someone else's feet,
by diving
into the opalescent pearl sea
gliding to the pink coral island
of the living dead beneath.
The fly by night
shadows
betraying
their natural born
solid twin.

And though the pale horse
bearing
the unbearable lightness
of the whirling boned
sythe swinging skeleton
with its formidable rigamotis ax grasp,
gaited through the once Arcadian village
after the Black Crafted
veined baneful
savage ravage.
In spite of this blight,
it was not hate
that planted the tear shaped seeds
for the young falcons
lost from their falconers,
to dragon teeth
resurrect
what they pained for;

But the memory
of velvet breasted Love,
revived by the fresh aerial breath
of the eyeless blue wind, Pegasus.

5
Armed with the sun glittering mesh
of a reinvented
symphonous
chiming childhood,
protecting
its cerelean uncalcified nest eggs
of endangered recollection,
directing the pack of sixth sense
scent sensing wolves,
their shared
key turning
the lock,
to wizard unlock
the mapped out plan,
now steeling their armor

sealing their feathered helmets;
as shadowless acolytes
slid through the Plutonian timeless tunnel
into the blind unknown
home of winding catacombs,
to reclaim the extinguished extinct
dreaming of apple blossom snowing petal blowing nothingness.
The efflugence of their blazing Herculean mastered wills
setting the River Deliver on fire.
The lynx eyed
animistic
dogged scrawny
bone trees,
Dog star howling
the deep guttural
language beyond words,
of the sleek dog headed boatman
howling his rippling approach
to the night is each man's castle, conundrum of moon seed bird legged offspring.
The Seer,
fish gliding through the spirit haunted water of tears,
eyes blue knife piercing the pitch of the speared cyclop's eye cavern.
Where slippery blind cave fish
poked up cat whiskered radar heads
sucking in the algae bearded water,
yet all thief cloaked
in tenebrosity,
rendering tendering
the pyramid eared ferry dogman
invisible,
only to be echolocation located
through the rythmic splashing of his oar.

6
Suspended by hooks
from the colossal
Gothic dome Cathedral
over the starless flame bursting river,
startled, bead eyes flashing open
in wrinkly faces,

the lice ridden leathery winged angels
of the underworld,
unsealing jagged Gothic wings
spanning
fanning the dense air
in nosy flight.
Gargoyle fanged mouths
screeching,
diving in
for a magnetic close up
of the usurping igniters,
the haunting hunting angels
circling
hostilely flitting at their heads.
The fever struck
purposeful
ardent children
heedful,
ready to react,
but not distracted
from the star struck
signature constellation
of their own design.

The eternal noctural aegis
nearing,
guiding the craft
sliding through windless waters.
Through the echo winding chambers
of his Anubis peaked ears
could hear
the feral Spartan orphans
barking
in his own tongue
witch they had sensed
was the spoken tongue here,
aware of the dogman's
penetrating presence
everywhere;

"O Pharoah of the neverwhere,
On our knees
we beseech thee,
Please
Take us to the fire eating
flame breathing sun,
cosmic dragon
mother of prismatic color.
The she
who be
both cannibal and giver,
for minus the empire
of the hissing dragon sun,
all is undone."

7
Elected
as subterrainean thousand eyed watch dog,
keen canine teeth
keeper
scent sensed
each hermetic sojourner
on this final hermitage,
who entered
the hollow belly womb
of the lichen dripping well echoing under world
Where he, the bone keeper,
windless glided in water winged legless chariot.
Made Lighthouse aware
by his head paired with blue topaz opulent reflecting eyes,
ebony fur rippling muscle armed,
golden jewel skirted,
royal loyal
Anubis descendant
the entrusted
ward witnessed
the hard rock crypt
under the stone lipped stairs,
cosmic dragon chose as lair

to lay her star bones within,
as she rose fire rose
transending boundless dimensions.
Believer of the children's crusade,
solidly came to their aide
delivering the gypsy strays
to the far side
of the fanged north,
by the mouth of the south shade,
to the cracked lipped shores
where the dead had finally died,
splashed the last of their tears
into the sunless River of Tears.
Arriving
at destiny's
black caped
destination,
Here at these furtherest
departing shores,
The electric energy mesh glowing children
 tipped the dog headed guide
by revealing in reveling smiles,
canine whetted fangs
matching this Anubis guardian's,
thus
leashing the dog man
to the bare skin halfling pups.
With paternal lidded eyes
he watched them exit leap
on winged feet
from the water winged chariot.

8
These vibrant vital sisters brothers
seeking the Phoenix resurrection
of the ambrosial bee sucking pollen dusting
fecund honey dew paradise,
infected by the virulent clap contagious plague,
brought on by the anemic blood sucking sisters

riding the fluid red horses of the sanguine tides
to the open shores.
These valiant haunted underlings
seeking to heal the sores;
Whose Camelot shouts
Narcississ echoed
through out
the vast
moist stone skin womb:
"Wake Up!
Get up!
Lift the stony lid.
O heavenly sun
thirst no more
for nothingness.
The blood rose Sun
must rise.
O ageless aegis
who rules over grow!
Show your
dragon shaped flames,
rage your waving claws
from the hole you left in the sky.
Rise!"

9
Then
Somewhere beyond symmetry,
prismatic energy
hummed
in earless ears
hearing shadowy elusive flute voices
dimly dripping, then rushing forth
bleeding their need
for the cosmic annexed  Phoenix
firebird
of all origin.
The one whose shade
of flames

licks away obscurity.
This dynasty of that cosmic dragon,
ignited minature suns
aroused her crucial return
burning through invisibility
a ferocious solar altar
spiriting its return.
From the end of the world
where  roots are cut
and one is no one,
a scorching blazing draft
shot like thunder bolts
into her star bones.
This furnace fury rushing through
the shaded pasts nothingness;
at last
blasting open an earthly portal.
Her orange and red fire buds
revitalized
by the flood of oxygen,
she scrambled clawing up
the wounded welkin,
Phoenix fire feather soaring
above the blue horse wind
who lost its lucid sapphire eyes,
and learned to hear
through conch shell ears
the angels in angles,
cerelean haltered
to the stable
of earth's
stone fire water air
and breeze nibbling green leaves.
The comet shooting cosmic dragon
hurri cane hurried
like four legged thunder,
steering with its meteoric tail
higher higher,
up up

to the hole in the abandoned sky,
circling
digging, until finally cloud nine nesting,
holy covering the hole
with primitive prismatic light.

10
Still wrapped within the last past,
Anubis,the thousand eyed
Seer, believer,
surrendered himself
to watch dog wait
for his naked pups'
dogged steps
leading back to the tugging ferry.
Poling the windless water winged craft
backwards from the ending
to the yawning entrance
with the halflings in tow,
whose pure ebony crow feather purpose
enlightened this flock,
So if the holy Anubis
weighed a feather
against
any of
the chosen packs'
chambered vessel,
the scale
would not tip
the balance.

11
Unhelmeted,
hair tossing
rabbit leaping
onto the verdant spear blades
sprung up beneath their feet.
Gleaming electrically

beneath
cosmic rainbow dragon's rays,
these Odyessy survivor children,
read from the timeless
Book of the Dead
witch was written for the living.
Scattering dragon teeth
seeds of wheat
witch when tossed,
the surreal cerulean cloud mane wind
pawed an opening
into the ground's
sucking mouth,
resurrecting towering
hydra headed stalks
for the brides and grooms
of the cosmic rubric dragon,
and the eyeless cirlean wind,
to harvest and eat
at the moon stockinged nuptial
of the extinguished extinct

when summoned by love
their spirits
aborted
from neverwhere,
flashed back.

Not to lay claim
to the old and rotting
hay haired
deserted
worm eaten corpses,
but to the scintillating new
temporal suits
waiting by
their decayed remains.

Their
now regenerated
energy,
fish swimming
into the fresh
carnal flesh temple
of sinless
sensuality;
unburying the clock's
broken hands
 set—
to tick tock
clock-
wise
again.

## AFTER AFTER

After the eyeless
blue horse
wind
was wickedly whipped
by the ghost rider,
rousing its remorse-less
strong head
thrashing tail winds,
snuffed out the wicks
dripped darkness.
Through the red orange green blue domed
pumpkin homes,
specks of mould
flecked
pestered the walls
rotted
slowly sunk,
festered
into an oozing puss.
Nightshade crept
its deadly fingers
tugged the nightshade
down
blinding the town,
seeping
poison green vapors
lingering.
Under the mushrooming
fungus spell,
wrapped
in ghost-ly
flapping gowns,
villagers sleepwalked
circling around
the dazed face
of the tower clock.

The Nightengales'
(no longer sailing
in happy-go-lucky gales)
firefly shimmering songs
were jarred,
bottled up
inside.

The cosmic scales
of harmony
tilted,
as the Celestial Sun Dragon's
scales
of crimson midnight suns
rained,
charring the scarred
children
below.

2
Prismatic rays of the blazing dragon
froze,
as it lightening bolt-ed
off the divine
cloud 9 hold,
tumbling until it crashed
shaking an earthquake below.
In the big air
leaving a hole
for plague ridden demons to enter.
Fanning her fly-by-night
Phoenix fire dripping wings
vacillated
as the eons and eons ageless, Celestial Dragon slipped
from the once Arcadian ocular, now vaporizing view,
crossing the jaded
shade haunted peaks
to the other side
of this steep purple Great Wall divide,

where snaking on its under belly
scrambled deep,
sharp cresent moon sliver claws
shattering scattering rock
coalminer digging
into the starless bowels of Middle Earth.
Egged on by the recoiling dragon's
now refueled flames,
tail
coiling around
cave skull cavities and giant rock teeth,
furnace heating the goblin labyrinthing tunnels
network mapping below Midgard;
So that even
in the far off Icelands,
the goaded volcano
boiled
pitching a fit
spewing out fierce biting
bits of black glass.
So that
transitioning from the baby fishermen filled turquoise silken star woven Chinese slipper
around the bend
to the toddler rocking wooden shoe silvery herring star filled boat of the west,
the Sandman
busy
fulfilling devoir,
while crossing the crashing day reservoir
between
on his indigo poppy seed sleeping narcotic
journey,
drifting twilight zenith aloft
was rift, cut to the quick,
his lining split
pouring beaches of sand
morphed into more glass and smoke
so living dreams were choked.

3
The arched back
stretching cat
Prism vibrant
arching rainbows'
pure colors were bled,
turning bad blood black instead,
at the beginning of the end
its Leprechan planted pots of gold
tainted,
turned counterfeit
lead.

During this groin howling panting Dog Star bristling
Mad Tom ranting
lunar lunacy,
everyone was alone,
dislocated ice-o-lated,
only out for himself.

Still loyal unfoiled
Spirit guardian gargoles
transfixed on the eaves
of the spiraling cathedral,
tasted, smelled, the firy Armageddon,
watch dog barked,
broke off their stone talon feet
to escape,
croak their deep throat warning.
Yet, in the attempted
still born
stone-d flight,
cracked down the middle
decomposed
into primal mother dust.

Due to the swelling beastial
pregnant squatting Yin

devouring the Yang's
promising smooth vibrant vermillion eggs,
the navigation of negative
uncircumcised circumstance,
led to the Bad Lands,
And
it was too late
forever.

4
War became the Satanic ritual.
Yet Satan was a Raven indigo winged angel,
though infamous,
an angel none-the-less.
Chains of
maudlin liquid beads
slipped from his mirror eyes
reflecting a rank army
of corpses
piled in his hollow honor.
Attacking their own torsos,
hacked off
legs with mutinous kicking feet,
arms with anvil pounding fists,
seeking unhinged revenge
against themselves,
admist a rising salty sea of blood.

Satan, backwatering
His black rainbow wings
arching flowing behind
Heaven's Locked gates,
where the tremulous angel hid
amid swarms of rose bushes,
but the savage thorns
stabbed out his eyes,
leaving him blind
as God less.

The harmony starved earthward angels
skeletal,
their pristine swan feathers
torched
in the funeral pyre
bursting flames.
Their heavenly array
now
elongated finger
bat flapping
hooked wings.
When they blew into their hardcore tanished
Gabriel horns,
ashes snowed out,
the music
mummy mummified.

5
Starcrossed
beasts
Lost
their defences.
Some species
carried during the apocalpse
were born
eyeless and hairless.
Fierce
bone trees
no longer
erupted from bald skulls.
Unicorns' ivory tower twisting horns
were shorn,
cut off
from their towering magic,
with blank foreheads,
they turned into pale horses.
Lantern green eyed
orange striped
moon tigers'

claws
slid into the slits
could not be unsheathed,
their dagger teeth
fell out.
Hunger and despair
out foxed
the blood stained foxes
unable to hide
crouched trembling
on barren cracked hills
where
Leafless hunched orchard trees
dropped shrunken headed
fruit.
Even the Blakian crowned Sunflowers
hung their huge
Martian heads
bleeding weeping seeds.
Under the skinny light
where darkness grew bloated,
only the corpse eating
beak nosed
vultures
also bloated
thriving floated,
fearless encroached
knowing no boundaries.

6
Besides the death winking raptorial birds,
deft and quick
stealthy wolfish
stalking
shark finned
bony night children
with bogey Golem eyes
survived,
by giving up

any pretence of pride,
ready to fall on their knees
lying spreadeagle
exposed,
managed to evoke
stroke some sense of pity
from the syphilyptic
epilyptic
ecliptic
empty pit
eyeholes
of the blind leading the blind
fueled
hard rock
crippled
tenderloin
cruel
crutchless
pendulum swaying
gravity grave
once tender,
slaughterhouse
rendered,
hard shell
renegade
Mother Earth,
wrecklessly
anarchistically
spinning off
her unanchored
axis ----

# THE SNOWMAN

There was a snowman
papa pack-
ed
rock and roll-
ed
from slippery black ice.
You'd think that would suff-
ice
to make him sneer, wanna' cheat
a grim tightwad sneakin'
Ebinezeer.
But No,
he was over the poser
side of pale,
a real
triple binding blinding white.
Yeti, he was
a snowman with a heavy heart.
Though naturally
left out
in the cold
illusory and vaporous,
snowmen a-parent-
ly are spawned
from jingle spirited lawns,
minus tick tockers.
What
without a rib vest around the chest
to hull
such a muscle thumper,
but if he did possess
a beating clock, witch of course he did
 metaphorically,
belonging to the quick and fleeting seasonal clock stopped
by the increased glare
of the intrusive sun,

glittering black ice
vessels
to carry snow wife, round children too.
And maybe vessel sail
motored by the old brain memory
through the Arctic or Antarctic sea
of the arctic polar sea
Cascading swaying
at the top
End of the world
or bottom,
depending witch end is up
(origin of the Snow monkeys, that evolved into a Snow people species).

This snowman under study,
with skeletal arms, twiggy leafless branches
poked through his torso,
supplied with Mother Goose splintered scary tales broom,
to sweep away doomy gloomsdays?
Maybe, for he was a snowman
that cared
shared empathy and  freezing sneezes.
Though earless
he could hear
singing voices everywhere.
No mind of barren winter had he,
nor was he made of hate
as in Frost's poem,
"But from what I've known of hate,
Ice is also great
and would suffice." Though he was made of ice
and Frost,
it wasn't Roberts'
but Jack's.

How now
Jack Frost's
number one
son,
inwardly complex

unique
as each intrinsic intricately patterned
infinity snow flake,
qualifying him
as owning
a soul
is
what makes you
different
from every-
body else.
His cheeky face
a melancholic glowing know about it,
witch hailed
over him
ice bullets,
emptying from the hard gray sky-Ratta tat tat
machine guns gunning
down
pelting
his bald head.
Instead he cunningly helmet war
traditional stovepipe hat
puffing curls of smoke
cookin' with concepts and dreams
his stiff branch hands tried to bander snatch
floating past, a barrage of lawless infinity colored moving movie reels.

No sparingness
for this arctic effulgence
crystallized
die hard
breathing frost clouds
luminous ice box
felt what seized him
to sneeze,
thus was hooked
by the bleeding feelings
melting him,
sweating profusely

leaving puddles at his feet less.
This black ice
snowman
who peaked
a dwarf less
Snow White
shiny wet.
His (Yeti gender assignment questionable, perhaps Abominable, if snow people be
androgynous, or do you know, is their sex equipment concealed under layered skirts of
snow)
carrot nose
robbed of its purple velvet dirt season, ripped root less from its root cellar home
lost from its flaming orange pointed v-nose rows of siblings
was hurt and vexed,
believing there was no karat reason
for its frozen exile.
It shivered shriveled like a witch's hexed finger
defeated but
Halloween lingering, losing its hold
in the moaning sub zero below,
a death camp for carrots.
Though the snowman was climatized
and did not hunger for food,
there was some beard less snow less
thing
he did hunger for.

He saw it reflected in the diamond faces
of the snow deer wearing branches on their heads,
glimmering in their amber planet eyes
as wagging flag tails they leapt
into the trackless
tracking the leader.
He thought it rhymed
with glove,
like the knitted fingers
the boy wore
to throw snow
balls.

This absence thereof
felt like a black hole
or a deep lacuna
even though nearby
the blood red poinsettias
bloomed in full blast.
It caused his coal eyes
to smolder orange red
the chin less snowman's
coal mouth to curve into a fallen
smile less
burn like a furnace
embers ignited by the fire of desire.
Sticking out his tongue less
he wished he might taste
that rhyming word.
O his fierce heart less
a hungry gorge!

The proverbial pipe he held in toothless mouth,
unless you could claim
the black coal
now seized by orange
as teeth
ignited his corn cob pipe
began to pop corn  pop pop pop!
A tumbling heated fountain of crucial substance
for any wandering winter fauna,
except the poor ice man's
glaring staring eyes
and mouth
engineered a rain of terror
he never Ivan the Terrible chose.
He was kissing cousin
perhaps
to the crucified man
stuffed with straw
painted with a Frankenstein face
resembling rage, terrifying the ebony sleek feathered bead eye friendly crows

that the straw man perceived as the rightful indigenous inheritors
to the yellow teeth corn, worm home ruby apples, black olives that fell in the fall,
but his apocalyptic
mask
ripped off their wings,
held them at bay.
Both of these sweet monsters, not deserving
the inaccurate service of their fiendish appearance.
Neither either knowing the how why or by whom they were created,
Nor way did they manager manage to tender-
box
the look of twelve angry men.

This malnourished glittering black ice
peaked freaked out to Snow White
man
with his block solid ice conscience
also
had been had
by the screwed up
dis-ease,
pivoting OCD formula
cause and effecting him
to feel responsible for the why around him,
believing all reflected
what?
the snowman perceived.
His desperation about the hunger,
reflected in the long bleeding fingers of the sky
scratching to snatch onto the disappearing illuminati.
He tried to save the dying light
by tediously untying
the knot in the scarf
with his stiff rake like fingers
that someone had tied around him
hang man style,
tossed it over the light
like a life preserver
to keep it warm.
He then extended his rigamortis hands, reaching out to the bleeding light fingers,

giving the dying day a way to
jump rope backwards into the earlier illumination,
but those flaming fingers slid away
and the ghastly ghostly black void sky blanked out.
When the shining ice cubes froze blue in their circumference
continually tilting like an hour glass over earth,
he stoked up his stovepipe smoking top hat
so they would shake down from the sky like melting dice.
Using the dueling fuel power of his hungry gorge heart less
he shot off flares
into the galloping night mare night.

For he was the ice man
cometh,
a fighting man
who would not rest
from his fiery zest
to make the world
right as rain,
spring up again
going backwards through the forwards of time
in the Einstein calculated after Math
defying or complying with the odds of March
as a solo Decemberist

under the emptying trays of ice cubes
ricocheting off his head cover
stovepipe hat
beneath the ice beard
reign
of the weird dead less
a mist
this nihilist
cubist
ice box world
searching for a God-
less
at the beginning of the end-
less
friendless.

## THE DANCE

My head is an egg
my hands are branches
my feet are stones
my thighs and legs are lame,
still I am a dancer, I dance the dance,
when the spirits charm my body
I am light and lively
and my hands the little green branches
are blossoming with flowers
and the sun pleases them.
And my two eyes they do not sleep
when what is behind me
is the moon
I wear gloves of the skin of the moon
is a fish.
O I am not with hunger then
or with wanting for anything,
And I am the dance, I dance the dance,
myself I do not lie down,
I follow brightness beyond the hills
and bless the earth I walk upon
the stones, the braches, and the egg
anointed by the rain
I shall go without a name
into the shape of an egg I am.

I dance by day, I dance by night,
removed from all complaints,
until the spirits end their spell
leaving behind
me,
broken shell,
with sorrow
and a sigh
when I come back again,
when I come back again.

# WHITE GOBLINESS MOON

Abra cadabra!
White Gobliness
Moon's
Mona Lisa
Bold
Highbrow
eye brow less
full
staring face,
Slides a head
In the twilight shroud.
AIEEEE!
Holy white blood
Stigmata
Spilling.
Anarchistic ally artistically
Glowing
So, nobody sleeps tonight!
Surfing surging
Steeping leaking
Through open doors
in the velvet gloved
gentleman
mole's head quarters.
Labyrinth mazing
layers
Underneath
the hedgehog
Green spiked
Grass mass.

2
Here, in this moldy cozy
Numinous luminous
Moon stung stingray
hallowed hollow,

dwells
that old tubular
grubber.
The grave and shrunken
Root Mother.
Galloping her tendril fingers
Tenderly poking and prodding.
Old nursy maid
Caretaker
Covering
sleeping seedlings
In her charge,
With an xtra layer lair
Of pajama dirt.
Electrically connected
To the dazzling
Steed
Un shoed
Hurling
Moon fury.
Her button hooked eyes
Unhooked
Slide open wide
Charge on,
Blink
Wink goblin mischief.

O daemon skimble skamble
Drop the thimble
Miss a stitch
Prick a finger
Ouch!
Goblin suitor
The moon's spittoon,
Metallic armor
Suit
Reflecting amour
For his

33

Rock Candy
Mountains
Boozing fountain
Mistress.
That old
Gluttonous goatish
Satyric moon.
Swoons
he
Slips into the pond,
Wraps stubby arms
Around
her
Mooning
him
Having sex with water
Mooing
him
Drowns.

3
Egged on
by wise potato chips
wisened
Blind potato eyes
Now far reaching
Yanking
Stimulating
Monkey tails
Twisting dangling
Obscenely
Hanging
Spying through
Tendrils swelling
Waving elephant like
Trunks.
Poking noses
Into living secrets
Of the dozing never dead

Furtively glossing
hoodoo voodoo
calcified streaming
scratching
trails
Of curling
fingernails.

Get out of my hair!
Rivers of flowing
Green tresses
Growing.
Horn thorn
Black bud
Roses
Blooming kisses
(from the Guadalupe Virgin)
In emptying suit lapels
Or bouquet clutched
In knobby knuckle
Fists
Over emptying dresses.
Mr. and Mrs.
Worm eye,
Wedded in
This prevailing unveiling
Living dead
Virgin myth
Bliss.

Gloating
As they
Couple,
lay back
On satin pillows.
The true loves
Rock and roll,
at least
Turn over
A new blue leaf.

4

Come on
Chant the goblins
Eating both later
Of upper and lower crusts.
Monkey with the root
routing
Old potato head,
In your carousel carnival
of blinking
Christmas
Eyesight.
You turned on
Xmas tree
Symphony of eyes
Surprise!

Mismatch
Crosshatch
The crossroads,
Evolutionally
Religiously
Formulated
for
Herbs and herbivores!
Then
Earless
Old Mother Hubbard
In the hoopla hub
root cellar
Cupboard,
Cross breeds
Recipes
of species.
Her blasphemy
Smacks of God.

5

The smiling skull
Smoking eye hole
Skeletons
Applaud
Jangling their piano keys
At her spasmatic spits
Of sarcasm and wit

As she Multiples the pods,
So seven
Is even
And eight
Is odd.
Stupid
Is
brilliant
And stooped
Is tall.
The old grubber
Wears a wizard's
Lightening
ziz zag
Dunce cap

Old
comfy and nodding
Grubby nursy,
Conundrum
Condom less ly
Confucius
Confusing
the earthen womb
Groans
Her gnarly births

6
Hamming it up
That sweet old
Yam
Tickling with her galloping
Trotting prodding fingers
relishing
The seed and pod green children.
That hatless
Stuffed potato
Whose buttoned eyes
Buttered up
Winkie Blinkie
Open wide
Only
When
The Holy
With sarcasm,
Chasm smiling
White gobliness
is
fueled
and bad blood
bled

and inside the pregnant mare's
rippling belly,
the four goal
white mule
foal kicks
a rare
hybrid.

# SUPERNATURAL UNICORN (DIEGO POEM)

O zero hero,
Venus fly trap
 snapping up
vampire blood sucking bugs
that plague our naked species.
Puck inspiriting
juicy pink meat grapefruits,
green red golden globes
hanging by a curling finger,
in the meadow larking meadows,
the orgy of color, vertiginous ears
of dewy shivery buds.

Umbra umbrella winged Diego,
his rapine paws
a muskateer trio of white star flickers,
one paw wearing the absence of light,
the inimical force of nothingness.
Regal Jackal Egyptian ears
sonic over sized
releasing heat, panting tongue
cooling capillary circulating blood,
speeding this survival, revival flow
his enviable
surface to volume ratio.
So no sandman's seemingly deserted desert
slithering golden snakes, Scorpio scorpions, marble eyed mummified  toads,
burying themselves, taking cover
from the vulture raiding sun
hovering above, the ragged sky wrung of moisture,

No No Man's  Death Valley too immense,
as his mirages reflect back
Real
cool lucid pools
papayas and milky coconuts,

balmy octopus palm trees
flapping elephant ear breezes.
His bravo tenacity, ululating soprano voice
shattering wine glasses.
His bulbous skull
encasing the amazing intrigue
of his mercury quick silver brain,
creating him inviolable.

Thus and so
his velacol raptor raptorial heart,
fork and knife meat slicing teeth,
star studded ensign assign him
as King of the fury, eye of the hurry- cane
furious funneling wind.
The blue feet beach strolling, lulling breeze
that was zapped, into a monster head wind,
after a fateful star crossed meeting.
The gyrating boy-stir us blast,
street trick tricked, by the spicy iron maiden,
offering herself up for grabs.
The wind swept off its feet
reeled in, enticed,
presenting a nose gay
of poppies and rosy posies,
for the sweet heart,
a heartless breathless breasts sculpted
false bodiless cover,
the innocent wind, mingled within.
Trapped inside her harloting Venus
curvacious shaped sarcophagus,
seductively painted female disguise
a device wicked cage.
Its spiteful doors,
torture prison locking up,
spiking transfixing the blood paying customer,
nailed by penis penal-
servitude,
on entry of the lecherous john.

In this distressful case,
the bogie pent up wind,
flailing wailing, bolted within.
The back bitten wind, fuming volcanic vengeance
short fused ruse
imploding exploding,
sinister splinter aborting the box.
Its escape enraged dragoon maruding violence
World War Three apocalyptic.

B is for bat,
D For Diego, Dog spelled backwards is God,
quadrupling inimitable parts of his
unlimitable
fusion synergy energy.
His tintinubalating prowling howl
seizing the combustible reins, of the colossal top spinning winds.
Quelling, nipping its spurned spurred ire,
with his cold blood ignited, ice flight wings
circulating blizzards, slushing hushing the fire
of the irate cyclops eye
fueling the tunneling funnel,
feeding it spoonfuls of ice
silver spoon balanced
between
the unshoed unshod toes
of his dime sized feet.

Virtue virtual reality
Pancho Villa commissioned,
as King of the disputing brooding seven
squid inking
greedy sucking, undertow drowning,
sharking, giant tortoise biting,
massacre stained fighting seas'
convienent bubble head conscience
absolved dissolved,
spindrift blown
over a plunging argosy of sinking heads,

mutinous pirated seized
Ho! Ho!
by the amnesiac "suffering" rogue seas.
Diego the mantic manta
ray
of the God Dog Bat,
riding the seas' towering, turquoise horses.
His starfish heels, black inimical paw
spurring stirring, ponying the surge surf onwards
to the blurring turf of the wave horse coral corral.
The capester winged cowboy
slipping on handy doggle goggles
over his rich ruby eyes,
flipping off the white cap curving horse's head
into the duck footed flippers, oxygen tank fathoming banks.
These tooling aids, mirage projected,
strapped on scuba shielding him
as he congenially streams out bubbles.
With the heart of a sperm whale,
his indigenous motor spinning tail,
his rapine feet, doggedly digging
kicking up a slew
of the sea's, dragon hoarded booty.
Silver and gold, blood rubies, fire opals, crystal diamonds,
dark and bone white pearls
bunked in surfacing trunks,
water shrunken, drunken bobbing heads
floating up as absolute proof
of  wink of an eye, hood winked savagery,

revealed unpeeled
with one diminuative dime size thrust
of his sluth truth sluice juiced paws.
The seven rapacious seas
guilt ridden, forced to see
memory perceive, the exhuming of treasure stashed caches,
murderous slashing binges, legs feet hands waving
upwards
limbs swimming,
not to mention, the seas', artifice of head shrinking!

Creeping away, awashed abashed with battering shame,
water tiger ferocity, velocity tamed
by excess of gruesome evidence
composed by the little snaggle tooth,
Sherlock Bones.
For unmatched briny bravaura, quid pro quo bonus, a silvery giant Tuna
the armored tortoises ripped off from, a Cadillac finned, streamline dead eye frenzy
feeding shark.
The tortoise's, fed up with the rifling seizing seas'
forever never coffered wrath,
slapping the green plated shingles off
their head and limb dome tucking homes.

The embarrassed seas, bare ass exposed
forced coerced to wear pants, cum uppins, for the raping and pillaging
head shrinking, raucous rogue flings,
sacking the psycho seas' ruthless debauchery.
At least until later, when the training pants
are kicked off, ripped to shreds.
When again, splashing through the kelp
sea umbilical summoned,
bronco riding the seas' white horses, Pancho Villa style,
chiropetra  barking king beckoned
by the sea snails' bubbly slug slimed
Help!
Ringing rhyming in Diego's, elephant huge heat emmitting ears,
until his fearless paw of, the inimicable force of nothingness
punches Judgement Day, into the maruding mudering seas,
bowing before the bow wow crusader,
smoothing the wrinkles, stretching to earthquake towering Tsnamis,
halting the seas', far reaching wrecking ball, pulpy, polyp green hair raising range,
ancient trolling, racing raging face.

The Puck sucking, flitting bee pollinator,
a black sun to the crocus stars
oragami folded shut
intered in the blue vault of day.
Flapping his ancient, bee size, leathery teradoctile wings
he navigates the black paw meridian,
igniting the dilating stars.

41

Enthused, infused
after the moribund, sanguine girl
who lives in the golden rocket sun, descending below
the monastic snow robed mountains,
opens the flaming door.
She steps out into the polysonic world,
hypnotized mesmorized by the cymbal crashing river,
Ophelia drawn in
sizzling waist wading,
slipping beneath the smouldering sanguine water.

Daring Diego, sweeping staring
into the far seeing, faring stars.
Aviating the aiming imago, indigo gloaming,
Venus fly trap
snapping up bugs.
Little domino dynamo king
of whom the totemic roaming
hunger hustling, bristling wolves sing.

At the supreme sight of whom
pike eyed owls
hush their hunting shrieks,
release from steel hook talons
squeaking violet crowned mice
tumbling into thick, wind pressed, buoyent layered fields.
Their bald pink pap suckling babies
hungry, surreptitious den waiting,
for the seed nut and flower
cheek stuffed parents,
pink ears, nose sniffing, scared straight tails
now safe,
mother's ambrosia nozzles dripping
as she nears the peeking castle rock.

Diego at home, in his sky light domain,
three mini Cerebus six eye heads
Jackal perked ears,
dogmatically on guard.

Swift black arrow shaft flies
ankle nips, the unfortunate
not reading the posted
Danger Dog sign.
Non heeding non receding strangers,
affronted confronted on the steps
by the shaking, snake fanged
growling blender,
zero hero.

Crow perches on my shoulder
to pharos better protect.
Drolly rolls, belly exposed,
fawning at his human pack's feet.
Sleeps crushed against my violin too high strung body,
unwinds listening to his snuffling puffs
Lilliputian zzzs,
and the faithful
jelly roll lull
of his soporific breathing.

The gypsy wagon lantern stars
wheeling across, the odyessy of space's open space.

O lustrous one,
unreined with the celestial ordained
bone star heightened, Pegasus,
wings transfixed between
Cygnus and Aquarius.
Traversing the layers beneath: the dreaming necked swan, the Aquarian maiden bearing
water to thirsty, coruscating immortals,
the red star, Ra invading, worshipping praising blue planet, of stretching breathing borders,
its morphing vaporous clouds rubbing noses, wearing dragon, dog, bird, puffy hippo shapes
for tellurians engaged in cloud gazing.

You unicorn, never straddled saddled, bridled, spurred or whipped,
keeping clear, not too near, exiting quick, when hooving across man's warden prison camp
devouring circuit.
Though perhaps allowing, a feather weight, cadmium dandilion crowned,

honeysuckle child, standing on ballet steady toes,
with star boned wrists and fingers, to tenderly stroke your mantle nose,
feed you a blue rain kissed apple, if it pleases you,
while you stood, tail, back haunches facing the beckoning woods,
ready to turn and launch, into its age old camoflauge.


Unicorns innately benign,
aligned with unmuzzled awareness, for the minute deserving and fleeting
leaf nibbling worms, beetles, crumb trudging ants,
and the early of most species,
hosts of earth's, virid ivy heart climbing twining, vagabond train trailing, green tux wedding.
O new age, medeval aged unicorn,
ushering in not evil,
but delivering amity, comity.
Your cat capering lion's tail,
aphelion migrating, storm steady,
limitless composed latitude
radical sky gypsy wingspread,
of Leda's birch white feather white swan
trumpeting its sly arrival, where she nakedly waded, in the diaphanous waters
of a mirroring swan lake.
Blazing with the eloping virile impetus
infused with the zodiacal zenith Zeus,
whose kaleidoscopic telescopic eyes, nirvana illuminated
by Leda's nacreous breasts.
Drawn to her blue shadow waltzing eidolion
encompassed by the magnolia purple, ornithic teetering, wrinkly feet grasping fingering,
sky bobbing twigs, a sort of rocking feather tail horse
for the sky vaulting earless , finger throat sized, spontaneous chorus,
of a teary dew maroon sky trembling forest,
heart sister to a young dawn demoiselle.
Of the solar electric, rabbit fecund, spectrum hearted, sorceress heating, healing evanes sun
in transit, to reach the other pearl side of the world,
fiery ears fading as the scareless hare, sun sky hops
across the green marine twilight, allied vapory bird woman, mother of all,
the stars her glittering teats,
searching for her green hair waist deep, sunset lost daughter,
beneath the crocus bursting stars.

O the young Madonna, of a new feathered human swan species
sperm stroked into being, by an artifice straying shape shifting God,
fluttering within the calcified oval transitory home
of a cosmic dome,
witch Leda birthed from her uterus.
The egg calculating, expanding
with the magic diameter of the child's growing bones,
the swelling pregnant egg,
bundled in the girl's skirts,
knotted at Leda's swan lake neck,
suspended against her phosphorous green
slim as a leaf stomach and waist.
Green nourishment dripping
from her virid swirling nipples,
as the demi god's swallow tail butterfly flitting
surges to kicking, against the egg
cracking like the Sistine chapel ceiling,
unsealing her feather wing glory child.

Only the unicorn's equipoised  feathered extensions
recondite eradiate equilibrium
balancing the macrocosm,
photosynthesis stirring the luminosity
of crocus bursting stars,
as he crescendos through the vertiginous odyssey of space.

The cavern mouth glimmering stalactite
erupting narwhal twisting
mermaid mystic prophesy gifted,
orphic pharos horn, third eye centered,
arcanely cuspid towering
through his thick equestrian skull.
Not used, misused as a massacre piercing lance
generated by a spiteful animus,
yet to luminous moth eye lighthouse lead
those on the Orphic Phoenix feathered journey,
away from the lean rib vested, snapping jaws winter
where only the evergreens and early arriving vaporous bird
mother twilight, bearing her star torched tribe, constellation children

within her diaphanous breast, illuminated star flecked boundless wings
glow green.
Reflecting across the aphelion Ice Queen empress empire
O lady made of snow, whose gray eyes, stare tunneling ice storms
through young girls' maroon green rocking horse feathered forests
like a surfeit of the seas' white horses
before they crash, pounding on shores.
Freezing the sun's green rabbit paw
thumb
bunny fecund springy sphere,
glazing white the unicorn dripping horn trees.

The unicorn's Hanukkah candling horn
benevolently gleaming through the pale gloaming
burnishing furnishing knighted light
for the traversing argosy of spectrum feathers.
If one of the small beaked  species
is too weak for the sojourn,
feather weight tumbling like a melting snowflake,
the quick silver unicorn, looping and swooping,
to catch the fainting star
on the broad horizon of his back.
His indigo empathetic eyes
flaring beneath the the whirling Martian red neighboring planet,
navigator returns with the rider hitchhiker
as he pilots through the mapped airway,
a hybrid brother of the translocating fated birds
and Leda's swan conceived cosmic egg son.

Sentinel leaving, his diminutive bead eye beaked brothers and sisters
reaching their octopus palm bole station
destination mango tango
sun shade striped
flock  beaches,
domicle from winter.

Rekindled, the unicorn, tapping his hooves,
curvets, eagle swoops, headed for the Temperate Zone

on his reverse route returning home
to the unicorn horns dripped from ice storms
hanging from albino furred trees.
Blessed by the rabbit sorceress sun
fluid vernal equinox rays, infused
by the stroke of her green paw
on his equestrian skull,
so he does not tremble and shake
when the white wolf winter
bites at his prophesy form.

So why? In the thread woven tapestry
made before the unicorn became extinct,
the castle roofs garrets and banners
painted tainted blood crimson,
empty slit eyes, numb stone dragon back ground
sloping at the hilly horizon.
Massif dazzling white mastiffs
manicle slave collars buckled about thick necks,
venal Cerebus lunging at the acumen
unhorsed except by tumbling birds,
paramount pure unicorn,
pharos guardian of balance.
And the castle huntsmen
dressed in their massacre color attire,
one blowing the horn, severed from an animal,
savage spear heads, transfixed at his pulsing throat,
artery throbbing swan exposed neck,
the hunts men too dense to know?
O paramount unmounted gods gifted horse
guardian of balance,
blessed by the fecund rabbit sun,
the vaporous mother bird of night.
O he is a gentle albatross,
an ally in the service of good
if they spill his blood,
his enemies will deliver themselves
to destruction.

And where is the Madonna Leda,
the refuge purity
of her purple waltzing shadow forest
to hide the gifted guileless animals.
Where is her bird man son,
and Zeus who fathered forth
the  demi gods,
and protects the unicorn's manifestation,
this medaeval halcyon force,
lacking in evil,
who dost not thrust, his forehead's towering sword
into these hounding, threatening, creatures.

## PUMPKINS

Very slowly silently suddenly
we grow glow
golden baby heads
beneath the blood red moon
its blood will fill us soon
fields and fields of us
our bald heads
peeking from the twining vines
our source the force

the sun our mother
her rays the food feed
our silk veins
the night is inside our mother
the silent womb
into which the milky way
spills
so we drink our fill
of the cosmic will
the perfect order of the universe
is printed on our walls
which strengthen with the coming fall

our thin lips drink our father water
who falls in the fall
as we grow he we need
our trans parent father weeps
as he knows we are going to leave
the vine
and haven't
much time

stars give us vision
our mother father divine drink
the universe gives us part of its mind
to grow we need think

next month you will take us from our home
in the magic field
where our heads have grown
and take on the task
to carve through our hearts
the features of alien faces
which will shimmer shivers,
they're our death masks

for Halloween is our last and fast past—

# THE COSMIC CRACKING EGG

1

After the full blown
Blowfish horned
Thorn bush
Swarming
Thistle and briar
Born
Rocket pot eye
Scarred and marred
Moody moon
Infecting
Interlude

The
Melon-
Choly

Plague,
Tightened its mortal coil
Incubus succubus
Sucking the juice
From the midnight
Lu lu loon
Moon
And vaginal swirling
Dawn
Generating
The genital squash
Was squashed.

Birds dropped
Their feathers,
Molted bald.
Cygnus the swan
Firebird exploded
Imploded.

Burned out blown out
Starfish dry bone
Sucked out.
Wizened,
Shrunk
lets go
its Yin Yang grip,
cornet tail plunged
crashing from its ripped space
in space
Into the hungry flashing
Waiting
Watching waters.

2

And a dark crystal
reflective Breugel
painted
Icarus,
wax feather wings
Cannibal licked
By his death star

As he
Satan fell from grace,
Plummeting
Head first
To be gulped
By the same pulsing
Slashing green witch
Finger wagging waters.

The red and blue horses
Dutifully dragging plows and wagons
Whinnied, cried out
In panicked alarm,
Pointed their ears
And muzzled,

Stomped giant hooves
Reared in fear.

But the nearby
Dried mud
Mummy wrinkled
Peasants
Looked away,
Ignoring the cursed dare-

Devil
Act.
Mindlessly
religiously focusing
On their own
Raking
Hay bailing
Backbreaking
Chores.

3
The sky wore a mask
Of ash
Blending with the peasants apathy.
Roots shriveled
shrunk,
lost their hold
in the underground cellar
as plants and trees toppled.
Even the cosmic orange pumpkins
Were sunken,
Those goblin horded gourds
Symbols of the bloomed
Harvest
Looted booted.
Striking the same
Deep melon-
choly
chord

over the land,
Love in the mist
Spiked
Devil in the bush.

And after this
Brush tendril
Captured,
Tainted painted
Betrayal
Of simple complex
Pisces fish
Leapt from the cosmic cracking egg

Transfixed
Belly up
Skewered
below
On thorn piercing bushes.
Like Christ nailed to the crucifix,
Dracula impaling his hapless victims
On spiked pikes.
Possessed by the incubating incubus
Succubus spell

Sin-

tillating
Bat winged
Angels,
slipped through the heavenly clefts and splits,
splashing into the writhing deluge
nailed to the green foaming waters
They melted,
Unable to Believe
in their own rebirth
Ophelia drowning,
Singing yet.

4
The moth man
Planning to inform
Other
Out of step
Angels,
Spread his ragged
powder thin wings.
Reaching the unyielding
hard hearted heights,
To fall powerless
back to earth,
Lying paralyzed
spent
In the dying fields.

Interplanetary
Symbols of divisible
Love,
The Gemini twins,
Pollux, sired by a God,
Castor, the sperm
Stoked stroked
Son of a mortal,
were split
by Castor's death
which carried him
in cloud wrapped shroud
to Hades
where he drank Lethe's waters
of forgetfulness.

But Pollux's unbearable cross
Of loss,
Caused his perpetual weeping,
Catalyst to
A milky film
Of cataracts,

Ate his eyes
Away
Leaving holes
So he could not see
Beyond the bleeding stigmata
of his lost brother.

5
Seized by the perverse
Current
Addictive attitude,
The morning Star
Consumed by the
Mourning plague,
Dulled dimmed
Eclipsed.
Its bones of light
Lay broken and scattered
Pray.
This midnight hours pre-
Veiled
As black dog
Gloom beasts,
Drive their
Funereal
Rocking
Chariots
Across the sky doom.

Mean-

While
On earth
On a stone dolmen
A Salem daughter
Was slain,
In a backwards sacrifice
To the radiant sun God.

Yet this ghastly
Misinterpretation,
Using violence
To restore the balance,
Caused the reverse magic,
Tilting earth
further
On its polar axis
from the solar source.

The perverse worsening,
A psycho-
Self revolving
Saturn,
devoured
His blinded by love
To the truth,
Children
Gnawing chewing off their heads
And helpless dangling parts
With their meat stuck in his jagged teeth.
Thus
Bad blood
Saturnated saturated through the ground
Flowing into the deceased
Awakening
As the living dead.
After clawing through buried layers
Beginning a ghoulish
cannibalistic reign.

6
The surviving human tribe,
Smearing ash
Squeezing grass mud berries
Blood
On their fingertips,
Tattooed wings
On their bony backs

In living color.
A craft
art –
ifice
of witch,
lacking actual
motion
served
as illusion,
fanning
only
their survival emotion.

# JUNIO GRASSHOPPER

Mr. Junio Grasshopper,
Although you are a leaping skeleton,
lime green exoskeleton
encasing inner organs,
you are not one of
The Day of the Dead
dancing,
hallowed holiday
revisiting skeletons,
but one of the green horned living.
Therefore, little wrinkle mouth grinning
armor casqued fellow,
Hop along Cassidy home!
Who are a musician citizen
of the blue hooded Santa Cruz mountains
peaking beneath the sweeping fire bird tail
of the sun
burning itself to ashes,
as the bulging eye
of the sky swimming silver moon fish
beams,
subsequently dissolving boneless
under the super vision
of the lustrous red astronaut sun.
But Beware!
For the carnivorous crow
wears the executioner's hood,
its bead black eyes
through the eye holes
see
with telescopic vision,
even your sensitized feelers
jabbing stabbing out
on either side
of the straw boater hat
that loving wife

patiently wove for you
from the dry bleached white grasses,
to shield your dry husk head
from the red ant stinging sun.

Mr. Junio,
one cannot be cautious enough
even squatting
through these long tendriling days,
And after all,
it is not beneath
these eat crow
pirate
thieving tweaking birds
to deftly pick you up
in tweezer beak
for a quick pick me upper
supper.
Yes! you would be
so greatly missed,
who are the dry horned
and helmeted
green centaur,
at the ants' weekly carnival,
inviting the trickling tickling
collective minded
royally hatched
crawlers
to climb and saddle you chirping
as you leap beyond leap years.
A thousand violins
resonate in your springing legs
aria vibrating across the dotted
bowler hatted night.
When you take to the sky,
your wings
the echo
of a waterfall.

Mr. Junio,
Please harken the heed:
It is almost July,
Fly!
Your humming summer mate
awaits your safe return.
Her earless ears
listening to the quickening steps
of the intruding twilight.
Her boneless dry bone nose
senses your tobacco juice scent
wafting on the zephyr's green tails.
Her near sighted eyes
strain to see
you,
o her knight in green armor,
in the fun house like
lengthening shadows.

Your very own
armor casqued
wrinkle mouth grinning,
bibbed baby,
who only has eyes for you,
shakes his dried pea rattle,
mad at the too long wait  for his dad,
bangs it on his daisy hatted head.
Sips dew from the bladed grass swords,
burps and chirps for you
beneath the thick moss beard
of the deep emerald forest.

Mr. Junio grasshopper,
Please heed the need,
It is almost July, Fly!
Your whirring wings
the shuffle of the dead's footsteps.
Perk your guiding antenna

radar sense the path
to the firefly twinkling moss village
by the clustering anacorous
floating white lily unwinding
blossoming pond
shhh shhh shhh
waterfall slipping
over the rocks
under the green lantern sky
of forever summer
where grasshoppers fan wings
to cool the perspiring night
transpiring in his dotted bowler
to walk across the star hooded mountains.

The towering bark
of the wooded woods
barks for you!
"Come home! Come home!"
Fire bird sun
is burning
her arduous tail to ash!
The stone fish
moon
bulges its silver eyes
to help you follow
the bubbling trail
the snail tail oozed
to your home.

The executioner hooded crow
through its mouth hole
scissors its sharp beak
as its shadow grows fat!
Don't fiddle around
leap fast!
The thorn thicket's
daggers

thickens into swords.
Mr. Junio Grasshopper,
summer is wasting.
It's almost July,
Fly!

# II

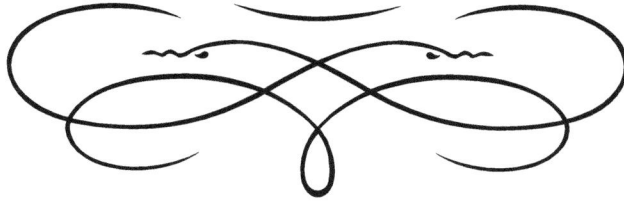

## LEAP YEAR

She
whose ivory key
Cheshire smile
chimed
the fishy
unassessed guessed
unbiased messages
of both
No and Yes;
was warrantably
handcuffed
by arrested development,
start gun
transfixed between,
being neither girl or woman.
Alone, with her nesting fingers
soothing stroked
wild and pinioned thighs;
then, as suddenly
as a mouse trap
springs
at the whiskery touch
of pink leaf paws,
Snaps!
the sniffy marauder's neck;
her rapacious
cage pacing panther
black heart
with bared dagger teeth,
furiously swung its mammoth paws
bent the bars,
squeezed between
broke loose
from the ivory ribs,
leaving a torched out
fathomless gorge

where her barbarous
heart
had been.
the special whirling black hole
its truancy left,
visible through her translucent
blue flesh.

Unchained from its leash
the en heartened heart
dumb bell
fell
to her feet
kicked off the heaviness
of its pumping organ
keys playing marching funeral dirges,
enough to drive anyone mad,
like an unappeasable unpleasable
crinkly wrinkly
old white haired baby,
its sailing tongue drifting in the wailing wind
a milk curdling scream
Waah! Waah! Waah!

2
How now
Blue with the rueful
mortal music,
her tender feet
and educated toes
broke off from her bony ankles;
the pink piggies
schooled in
magic realism
prompted
the died in the wool
deep seated feet
to Believe

in a Kafka guided
metamorphosis,
changeling into
two daisy eyed rabbits,
instrumentally beaten
to Rabbit Moon
Leap Year away!
And who could
blame
these Mercury winged
fleet wood feet
using minds of their own
to escape
such tone deaf booming abuse!

No feat
defeating her (at such an awkward age-less)
who could tame
no name to fit (Today Nepenthe, yesterday Finn, nothing stickling, again and again
if you get my drift)
penniless renting
the crutches
that propped up the sagging sky tent;
hobbled after her fauna transports
deep into the stocking hooded woods.

Her frog leg
jumping
thumping
croaking
sinewy muscled
savage
black heart,
in panther
panting
hot pursuit.

3
So over this,
mismatched
mouse paw mantle, orange orange and canary yellow
mixed up plaid
clan band
taking stage below
the far star reaching trees
dropping needles;

Night's
head of eyes
studying the trauma drama
through the moon man's globe,
with vaporous whirling sleeves
trying to grasp clasp it near,
shooting star missed
the di-
aphonous disk,
Nostradamus
visionary
priestial sphere,
moon walked
sliding backwards
spun
slipped
plummeted
from its Nirvana en lightened
heightened
pin up perch.
Swiftly sailing earthward towards
the quick silver horses wave flashing
shilly shallying
moon shadow mirroring roofs.
Soon soon
the goiterous emerald frog princess'
(wearing her emerald dew teared tiara
proudly throned, on a jealousy green
lily pad leaf,

in the warbling pond beyond)
silver ball
to crash
beyond the hard rock chimney
eaves dropping glistening homes.

Listen, can you hear
the moon shadow horses'
crystal clear eyes
icicle shattering
as the twiggy sky snatching fingers
miss the silver apple moon's
fruitless pitch,

smashing
glinting piercing pieces
scattering
through out the stockinged woods
still glowing
until
the moon dust
shimmering stocking
slides off
the obsidian Madonna's
thighs exposed,
now down on it
to the toes,
blacked out.

4
Hollow
grim faced
toothpick stabby teeth
biting
barking trees
steering into a lunarless piracy,
lashed and scratched
with gnarly thorn arms
trying to strangle

pray victim
hold
the foot less
she.

All was out to get her,
therefore sip
her trust
fund
ripped,
spilling gold
and green
mean
wiry legged
leeching
Black Sabbath
beasties,
flitting from deep Plutonic pockets
hidden in the freak show night,
dragging hatching offspring
still attached,
to ungrasp their birth grip and drink
at the buzzing salty blood feast.

5
And the ivy green hearts
weeping creeping
up the silver horse star hooves flashing
crashing into the moonless roofs,
and the ivy green hearts
weeping creeping across
the lobotomized lightless
hoodless stockingless
needle dropping
hearse cursed woods.

Though witch this gimping crutch limping
roaming
she who was not of girl or woman,

but measureless
gloaming
star dotted
see through child,
clutching raggedy button eyed blue rag doll,
rocking on a twilight spotted
rocking runner horse;
and some times was
 a crooked
wrinkly paper skin witch,
wearing sunless rimmed
conical black hat
pulled down to hide
her dim red eyes
already sheltered behind
corkscrew thick aunti sun shades,
witch nose twitching
tagging the rabbit scent
of her fugitive fleeing feet and toes
hopping through
the Nevermore
ringing
Raven winged woods.

6
Where the leaping good luck furry foot charms'
potent luck ran out,
ushering in harm
as unluck struck,
assassin stabbed and struck
devil may care
horned moon
honed
glass slivers
piteously piercing
acutely shooting

into the shrieking
surrendering tender

padded paws,
mutated translated
first one shoe drops
and then the other
rabbit duet
paused,
lost from the matrix force
mothering source,
froze in shear
uncut fear,
like ice sculptures
only breathing.

Over come with phantom limb pangs,
plus, the woe you know,
foster child fed
from abandonment issues,
she sprang rainbow whiskers
radiating echolocation
to further assist her,
witch hobbling footless led
to where the quaking orphan
orphic pair,
the healing father water
bathing his illusory
rabbit daughters (one Cinder ash Witching Hour
blood tears of the sun crowned nocturnal swan,
one ruby eyed, Snow White
as the rabbit moon
paunch
smiling against midnight furred grasses)
the osmosis liquid father
water licking, sealing their vicious gashes,
Opthelia reviving
his North of South lateral twins.

That brings us to
she
No longer

needing
the penniless rent
crutches lent,
duteously
returned the aids,
wooden legs
ladder stretching
to hold up the falling sky tent

7
This could be a Huckleberry
indigo glazed
ruby ripe cherry
dusk blue veined
rosary pea necklaced
Rose Mary's baby

blossoming new beginning;
But enough is never Enough!
in life's cunning as a camouflaged vixen's tricks,
As through the thrashing snapping branches
of the stockingless unhooded woods
her hungry heartless heart,
fat incubus
draining suffocating
unchained
rapacious
panther
black,
was feline whisker
Black Sabbath
stalking her,
and her moonless sable furred and snowflake rabbit quaking feet
To eat
ears flattened against heads
wept blood.

Offering the mercurial
crimson tulip eyed

non heeding non reading
red sky at morning
a sailor's warning
drunk
sailor moon sunk
footloose hoppers;
Rose Mary,
growing her black moonless
beam thirsty
dusk blue veined babies
budding, (rabbits are not cannibals of course)
wormwood
absinthe scented,
free spirited
indigo
rascally prickled
Huckleberries,
yellow Cyclops eyed, ballerina skirted daisies,
orange glo carrots
and other dirt layered
winding tendril fingered
root cellar critters,
exciting unpowdered pink glow nose
wrigglers, cloud scut wigglers.
At last
luring them back
with strokes and pats,
convincing her rabbity transports
to reattach (with the ambulance aid of an eight eye surgeon spider, stitching the ankle severed
ambulatories, back together with thread)
but they hung
like two noosed rabbits
with twisted broken necks
dangling in the raw-
hide stinging wind.

The now aupaired
savior faire
Huckleberry headstrong

lone wolf
maverick pair,
she rubbed
slipped and dipped
baptized by
that cannibalizing
bottomless abyss.

## ROCKING HORSE

Deep in the lobotomized
electric shock wave
sizzling
burned out light bulb
hollow leg
leathery tail whipping
choke cherry choking
"Never more," ringing
Raven winged
through sultry, even in the blank chill air
Aphrodite aphrodisiac
pulsing
sable stripper
Madonna
exposed

uncontrollable
madman, silent scream
vibrating deep throat
haunted engulfing
lost paths
crossing
fork in the tongued road
pathos exploding
stockingless hoodless woods.

Where
Overcome by an Orwellian panic,
delicate high strung
green leaf wiggling ear driads niads
suicidally leap
from their surfeit scented
petal stuffed
nook cranny niche
masquerading camouflaged
knobless

owl hour
ear hole
in the horned owl fortress
of their snaking trees;
as the seizure shaking vibrating
grandfather gnarled fingers
unable to clutch
slick slippery tongue
eves dropping leaves
shook off
shedding their crimson orange yellow wreaths.
Now winter bald
nuts trunks
unstuck crooked
crisscrossing
feet,
tore off
on tidal waves of fright night
terror,
like the swinging ax
hooded executioner,
had materialized
out of thin lawless air,
shouldering his battleaxe tinged
to woodsman chop
drop
the ring based
tree cloaks
timbering over
into fire licking pyres,
or felling selling the broke pinning homesick
punished
to slavery,
parts rolled off in carts
as tender box
kindling
to be ash smote.

2
Amidst this off key
hysterical anarchy,
She who fluctuated
between crepuscular star dotted
see through child,
and seething cauldron
froth spelling "Witch,"
along with her moonless
moon calf hare brained
iconoclastic
magic realism trained
pet trekking
reattached rabbity feet,
froze like the Dead,

that is, the rigamortis stiffs
later belated, evaporated from this dimension
(that is when they're not
Resurrection
Day of the Dead
but cooling their heels,
kicking up memories
in the swirling blue dust,
wearing flashing dream mask
gala costumes,
bones clone clattering beneath
as they fete prance dance
in bridal spider web woven
gowns and insect dream catcher nuptial skeins,
or black rose bud in the button hole
silken torrid night tuxedos,
or toredor
bull-
cape and golden button attire,
both genders wearing moon gloves
over their once rich coffee Latte Latin flesh,
now climate mummified
though their jet hair

painted
in still
sweeping growing strokes
These residents
of coffin city bungalow
underworld
where Thumbelina wedded
star nosed moles
with leathery blue webby feet
dig tunnels to China
North to beneath
this sir-
bourbon retreat.
Or continuing
in the venue menu
of true blue comparison,
and returning
to the furry hare brained shivery feet,
and the morphing She
froze
like a needly hedgehog
playing
freeze tag (except defenseless with no needles to throw)
or Edward Scissor hands'
sheared
sheer ice sculptures).

3
For
As the gossipy leaves
sticking out their tongues
lying
on the dirty needle
piled up floor,
out of a nipple knobbed door,
disencumbered cargo released
from the pregnant photosynthesis nursing
towering mother redwood
of its Trojan horse gifted birth.

The stowaway trunk escaping
moss streaked rocking horse
dragon's lair green
as a speechless Ozian night,
blinking eyes, summer green flickering fireflies,
furry nuzzling
muzzle seeking speech,
redwood
rocking chair ceased rocking
by the cobold kobold She
or it
who could not pajama fit
into any name
That same
measureless dusk dusted child
and the knotted twisting sun phobic witch (who felt she'd melt, vampire Poof! into dust
bared beneath closest cannibal star).
Both witch and measureless twilight ancient child
fetus curled pregnant with the other,
snapping together
like jagged maps,
helter skelter puzzle fitting pieces,
(even though the melon choly, shadow tailed and bonneted, elbow knee jutting,
sheen green witch
wore too huge
narrowly arrowly pointed
Gothic glaring button eyed shoes);
bewitched child
and witch,
entrails hitched,
wrapped together
stacked
like nesting dolls,
egged within
the autumn skinned outer She,
her nesting fingers
branching dancing off
within the wolvin wind wolfing night.
She, a lonely she wolf,

the swirling black hole
inside her chest,
dead star
sucking in visions
of the black tower
unicorn twisting horn
sword dueling
died tied tides,
of the bottomless magic top hat night;

with her opposite
north and south
of the Tropic of Cancer
dueling banjos
lateral polar
dazzling Artic
white bear,
Black forest berry bear,
salt and pepper
paired hare twins.
the polished imagine images
collapsed star
struck inside,
black light
x-raying back
their needle piercing
in living color
tattoos
cantering bantering across her air brushed
lampshade glowing
too thin skin,
where She stood rooted,
her rabbit feet frozen
in the heat
of the moment

Awed by what
the engaged
pistil

shooting
Bang! Bang!
into stamen
seedling
bristling into wiry pine cone,
botanically nurtured
neonate sapling caped
saw cloned,
across her Moscow Saint Basil
gauche tainted
ice cream swirling
unreal cathedral
carnical
reveling revealing flesh;
jack-o-lantern
ripe juicy
seedy gourd
layers
of debauchery,
fun house distorted mirror dreams
of the Breughel spoon in the hat
corn in the crotch
lusting crutch-
less crippled night,
wailing sailing through her
a vessel virgin,
no matter how double checkered
triple dickered
metro crowded
tumbling into red light district
her four legged sheet rumbling bed,
a virgin
that never
was
bridal suite
munching Munch's
perjuring
perspiring inspiring
fervor fever

in his painting "The First Night"
had been.

The firefly electrically blinking
green ivy hearted
red wood horse,
knock on wood
solid
in its lightness of being,
losing all sense of the grave
gravity
in the sit-
u-
ation,
winking its dazzling lightening green eyes
nodded,
for her with the misty rain
fog swirling hair,
and see through to the bone
Babylonian Nights prism inked flesh,
to mountain up
the sit.
In an unreined gained Renaissance fellowship
burying the school of hard knocks,
dead weight
rocks
rolled over,
piled up
piggy back,
while gossipy sharp tongued unranked leaves
swirled together in driftless piles
creating
crispy stairy steps
to hip hop
king of the mountain
eagle nest, climbing onto
the piano key grinning
green ivy hearted
red wood

vesper licked firefly wicked
rocking horse,
runner
rocked
kicked back-
wards
cradle rocking
Time
hiatus sleeping
ceased
fleeing fleeting,
seized a minute
seemingly an eternity,
hands striking
counter clockwise
to smokescreen aid
the Houdini escape;

just as the muscle bound heart
sprung its predatory lunge.

4
Acorn born
bursting crocus bud natured
rocking horse,
beating time
caught a musical rhyming ray note
ate it,
magic flute piper
pan goat
wood wind
blown,
floated up
over the grave draped
Jack of all
Spades digging woods.
She, cabalistically veiled,
with her rabbity feet
dangling

over the borders
of watermelon sunset east
and gold red coyote west, (nesting in night's moon less vest)
above the Grandmother red woods
towering cathedral horizon,
under the domain of the star nippled (to feed baby stars the shine)
eye opening
stockinglesss
strip teasing
Madonna,
eyes deep as the curving
compass less
dimensions of space,
embodying her terrestrial
charges
with bodiless
wide sky open
firefly blinking arms.
Electrically sparking
fueling
the wrinkle smiling
grass hopping fossilized shell ruling Mother
of crickets (including the golden caged singing pet ones too)
winter hearth conducting
with her wispy waving tendrils,
bobbing antennas,
"The Horse fly Sonata,"
her lime green skeleton
knee chirping children
answering
with touchy feeling horns,
in balance harmony
inspiring the Yen Yang
scattered
globe glass
shattered on the needly wood floor,
to magnetize attract
and eastward polarize,
coaxed by the swishing comet tail (like infinite birthday sparking candles)

of Hespurus, the wishing star,
moon glass slipper stairing, heavenly terracing up up the silver teeth smiling,
raven feathered renascent
nude balcony sky.
The Pan goat goading
woodwind piping
propelling the spell
to its lightness of being
gravity less
mare less hairless
woodworm inhabited
crane rigid legged
spindle to fat spoon moon blessed
green sap fed
shoeless runner
rocking horse
bravely moon cow baying
as the magic flute
blue moon rose
peaked over
his too tall
whittle sharp
rabbit hole echoing ears,
picking up the sharps, and pealing trebles
bi fold resonating
in the mood ring rimpling, genial fairyism, of the emerald tiered green lantern frog princess' pond.
The Hespurus raining grasshopper woods
levitating ceremonial key notes
by rubbing knees vibrating legs
flexing friction
unsealing pealing open crescendo growing glowing notes
to be glo worm read and eaten
by a wooden shoe sailing
dragon fly flying
flying wooden spoon horse.

As the blue moon rose
unanchored, balloon floated
to its premeditated, zodiacal zenith, Ishtar chosen berth,

straying toward the mane and tail sprayed golden drizzle (by the baby stars' glittery milk)
the mounted crusading horse
speared with his jack Rabbit free lance ears
the frog gloved
heavy lidded
Lily blooming princess'
silver Phoebe  ball,
jabbing it back
into its Ishtar religious
relegated calendar regulating
cup pouring forth,
cosmic spy glass
universal position,
full and satisfied
shine on Luna
Lunar ball
pinned up
over the toppled forest
spun back together
like a top
beneath its gravitational poetry,

Meanwhile
the perspiring tongue
panting ranting
rapacious
mean
panther black heart,
lightened up;
feeling tamed and blameless,
magnifying the unison
of the mermaid tailed
split hoofed Pan's
celebrating,
sea tortoise hundred year
cadential drum shell,
sea green legs, tail gliding,
whole pivotal moon's birth.
Plus, imitating the effervescent

innocence
of the wooden shoe rocking
glittering scaly fish filled
sailing
cradle rocking horse

soon soon
whisker whisking
wood come thumping jumping home
having endured a sacred savage
snarling alone
crimson poppy seed odyssey.

Along with the opulent
silky chalky
moon dusted
stocking
that was ripped
off
the holy night
space curving
thighs and legs,
regaining
with no tears and holes,
slipping over
now down on it,
from the thighs to the toes,
of the now luminous hooded, wise, Madonna lunar moth fluttering eye lashed, wooded eye browed
numinous lady.

And since
Home
is
where the heart
is
full-

filling
the suckling black hole

stitch less
closed
shut.

The black cat whiskered stalking heart
steadily bent back
the ivory bars,
to reshape
the cage
for its own safe keeping.

In finale,
the multi layered
melodious
She,
who would always be
a jigsaw puzzle
nesting doll,
beneath the tenebrous
bodiless body
of the star nippled tender Madonna night
feeding the shine
to the baby stars,
and to the nameless she
of the misty wet
fog drifting air hair

free
to leap
on her illusory
March hare
flying
whiskers
crimson tulip eyed,
blackberry black bear plush,
ermine dandylion fluff tail white,
oleander petal swan
pebbly river rushing
hushed rabbit feet,

to the crinkly leaf smiling
green bean shell
Mother of crickets, giving the signal
by bobbing antennas
waving wispy tendrils,
for the lime green skeletal offspring's
fortuitous symphonies (the golden net house blessing chirping pets, drawn in by the orchestral drift)
with two sets, her own pointy Doc Spock ears
and her pair of Loki rabbit's feet hears,
echoing the vesper harmony
erasing fears;
to the spring ancient blue amber emerald whirling Mother
of dragon blood darting dragonflies,
who bite the night
with chopping transparent wing blades
inviting the Hespurus wish
for the boy and girl stars
to run away
from dawn's rouge kiss

Charging over knife plunging
thick as thieves stabbing thickets
where buck teeth nibbling, Uncle Wiggly heart nose
brindled mottled solid rabbits hide,
rooted below the briar patch
where small cylindrical dug out mouths
fat flattened bunnies
squeeze sneeze
through
spiraling hollows
leading to dangling through the rood
juicy carrots,
onion bulbs' scented arms traipsing
through snug dirt rug rooms,
where fastidious bunnies
ears tied back with hankerchief leafs
sweep out mischievous dust bunnies
with dried palm brooms.

She (with her illustrious company)
astride
the mellifluent fluid woodwind
swaying through through the lunar stockinged woods,
glass horned Pan, goat furry thighs
shaking tail
slender ankles with dancing split hooves
glass holes magic flute piping;
dragon green lightening
firefly flash eyed beams
blinking
the lightness of its being
beyond grave gravity,
freakishly hatched inside the sap syrup belly
of a mountainous tree.
From tiny spiny bristly cone seed,
cloned infinitely
but not to create
another
sky elevator navigator horse (through never say never, the impossible is clever—
green sea rocking
muzzle stained
by the kiss of sap
cradle rocking
in the treetop,
Tommy knocker
knocking)
for the wind hiding its shape underground
to the roar up the tree
blow open the nipple knob door
to escape route
the mirthful terrestrial meteorite.

Through the woodworm glowworm
lit
hoary frost always autumn
smoky hazed daze.
She, a boundless passenger
on the Tommy knockers knocking

horse wearing rainbow glasses,
black swan feathered flight
through night's indigo swirling orchid
fanged mouth;
weather she is in
witch bent finger
nose itching twitching,
or turquoise looming
star clustered
see through child
eating custard,
or scorpion pinching
moon food;

wearing scaly moon gloves,
misty hair
waving swaying
curling curving
over the redwoods

horse.

# I, LAZARUS (Homage to Bast)

Gripping his bow, the indigo sweeping winged archer, who leaves no tracks in the snow below. Looses his lucent spectrum arrows, whizzing over the saber tooth ice fangs dripped from roofs; swiftly zenith soaring, to incite invite love's fireworks. But he is misdirected, blinded by the obdurate albino glinting squinting horizon. Lost in his winged compass footing, his ardent spells dispelling. For this is the haunted hamlet of the damned, and the corporeal inhabitants cannot be shaken awake, from their sleep walking zombie bondage. Domed under a darkling glass,the spurred like skeletal wheezing night-mares,spared not, for a breathing recess, chattel village, bells ringing funeral knells. Idleness invites the devil, neutered, bespectacled from reading the prattling "Son of, son of son of," holy battling Bible. Inflicting the conflicting "babies are born from the sin of sex," mangled genitals, preferably, Enos Eunuch castrated disciples. The hooded wizened face of the vagina,clitoris felon culprit slit, devotee stripped. So No body exults in the carnal, (fettered by pastoral priest netted, lepodoptera collectors. Pinning down nature's, opulent jaguar patterned symmetry, sapphire capricious, fluttering beyond borders, sanctimonious gold fringed pinions.) Foaming sea trusting, the pure lust of coitus and love. Dextrose vine entwining, Morning Glory radiant flesh towers fused, as one flowering force.

Lo! A poison arrow shot Cock Robin, through his Orphic dawn, downy, rubescent chest. Not one of Eros' tipped dipped in radiance, magic cupid arrows, but one strung by cruelty, released by a spiteful hand. A Saturnine assassin betrayal, like prodigal caped demagogues, robbing the phallus vulva dancing, milky healing amour, of the sublime climax. Subverted, converted by fear into nadir. Weary dreary Soldiers of the Lord, worker bee procreating, for the unhinged boa jaws, of the potent hungry, constricting church, to belly lump swallow more sheep. The steeple finger pointing, to a melodious milk and honey suckling, un-anchored paradisal promise. Confirmed, through belt buckle stinging rancor. Acolyte drilled, to sleeping beauty lay the true blue tiger hearted, rainbow genius, golden aurora baby, inside the penal dim coffin. Stuffing her waxy pink mouth with posies, binding her lithe little limbs with thorns and briars. Shutting the blind lid. Re-hatching a changeling, to replace the whirling pinwheel, neon blue thorax jeweled dragon fly soaring, exploring giggling dew glittering baby. Changed to a blurred lame chaste wasted, frantic fanatic. Remolded, remodeled by the predatory grasp of a malignant manifestation. The "Angel of Mercy," creaking open, the hidden below the lid, zombie baby body. Terrifying the screaming "beastial" child, tamed, into a castrated christian. Malign Angels prowling the beat, sucking black hole eyes, disguised behind paraffin, frozen smile masks. Snare hooks snatching, succubus lips eviscerating abdomens. These Angel cops, dragging away weak and stale bread hungry, pale Hansel and Gretel children. Who never, forget me not, got to taste the haunted sugar spun, cannibal witch's, candy house, pumping their gaunt little bodies to plump.

Snapping bolting jail sealing, stealing these delicate little flesh birds away, from any future feasting feasibility, of such spectrum glimmering gum drops.

A deified deathly deity, bankrupt never where fugitive stuck, pathos phobia of mine. Vengeful fiendish angels, I mean. And in this daylights' dwindling to lean bones of light, star flickering blank out, zero account savings time. The distinction between, fiction and nonfiction water color confluently merges. Not that two appealing, separate real meal meanings exist, without being twisted and hung from the meat locker hooks, before being chopped up. (In this Gothic stern zone, a reproving knuckled, branch hanging tree, for the dead meat, hacked, semantic divide, will meet the trick.)

And So much depends on the spikenard fenced century. Maneuvering, turnstile turning the gyring gleaming steel wheel,entering the station. Accustomed to the unabridged social customs, the prototypal protocol. Warding off pervasive, invasive, fleecing police. Granted the nightstick swinging clout, silver star appointed, to handcuff wrists and ankles. Inventing zooish, epizootic episodes. But from foregone quantums, provisionally, visually providing, the reforming badges of identity, restoring the hands off, "laisse faire" order of disorder.

In failing to procure a driver's license, or array of gay credit cards, do I cease to exist, subsist? Simply vanish into uncharted, Bermuda Triangle thin air? Or do I fugue stagger withdrawal, into an oblivious Plutonic ruled, Cat-atonic state, chained to the stained mattress, metal bed meddling frame. Electric prisoner shocked, under the condor flocked roofs, of Tom Bedlam's rat climbing cracked walls.

To avoid being detained in such les miserable grueling, watery gruel confines; in that identity crisis arena, (if you claimed yourself, it could be quite tame). (If a less cruel, hazardous, fuzzy mouse island ever reveals its squeaking velvety pink ears peeking pastures, I will hose squirt urine circle around its heavenly axis, markedly marking it as mine own.) Possessed by acumen, acquired from vivid cat-echist whilom lessons. I shoved my photo i.d. in wallet, deep down into, the back mouse pocket, of my blue plush pants. A top hat, Citizen Cat, buttery toast and marmalade at midnight, name christened, (provided with inside scratching post), slightly naive native. Cane strutting, gold chain, Stonehenge ticking pocket watch, tucked in front coat pocket, gentleman, with keen tiger claws. A tail most youthful hosts, were envious of, pretending to own their own bone instrument. On cubic zicconene flashing collar, a silver tag with address marked, pet.

Yet here in this cold as a witch's tit, "pit and pendulum," hidden diary, fire torched integer, no one owns such plastic proof cards, are poofed! Or spam. Home grown cats, orphaned (not by their Madonna milky dugs mothers), but in the absence of kind, human kind partners.

So for the trembling lamb moment, I am just a voice bleating bleeding through the sentient clouds. Not the barreling baritone voice of a gilded wreathe God, or a dead eye thriller killer angel; twin gold pistils, loaded with lead bullets, triggers cocked in holsters, slung on its peevish hips. Tobacco raspy, cancerous God father voice, ventriloquist escaping from its wax fake face, abrasive smile, coat hanger stretched, stuck lips. But my very own growly whiny voice of natal choice, vibrating through witch branded Salem. Hungry Kelpie unstabled , sneezing up from the remorseless bottom of the paprika seasoned, brackish blood Red Sea.

Where above the rock of ages eroded shore, the fire branding villagers, brandish hoes, pitch forks, and cudgels, at any unexpected "alien," daring to travel the unicorn shimmering green sea. Outlanders cited as harbingers of disease, and buzzard bald bold encircling doom. Crucifixes unsheathed from under cover plain clothes, to hold the "vampire" visitor at bay, so the unwelcome traveler, turns his vessel starboard, the sarabande waves trolling it away.

To counter act this flu struck, contagious demeanor, horseless stuck carriage, of the numbed, mushroom penumbra, throbbing veined superstitious religious. I rear up, curvet, scampering like a spirited pygmy blue horse, rebelling from its funereal clutches.

Here one must be leery of the bleary, mole dimmed eyes, reading by pining candle light, the Lilliputian print, meant to blind. "O rip out mine eyes, so I shall not give in to the crimson Devil with a cleft in his chin. His serpentine winding tail, with a pointed arrow at the end, his bestial self satisfied grin!" (Those stoking fires of Hell, Ahhh! Myself a gutter child, my toes stinging (lacking the proper Viking boots and wooly booties) the razor cold cutting right through my fur parka. What I would do, to lay my winter bitten self, by those fervent fires, and sunshine, hearth heart revitalize. Supple and limber again, circling in nocturnal worship, chasing my indolent tail, the unjarred stars looking on.

Well, as you are learning, compelled am I to exhume, dis entomb, crack open the lids of coffins, peer at leering skulls, with my shovel digging penchance to amble ramble. So much for training myself to wear the none habit of simplifying zen, as a minimalist, a nothing nihilist. The cat did Not, catch my tongue and tie it in a knot! That wagging instrument of flapping arbitration, word penetration, prefurs to wake, levitate The Lady of the Lake, from her watery grave, (for oracular communions' sake). Besides, all these turning, alley cat alleyways, stimulate the pink mice spinning, exercise wheels in my holy cheese brain. Witch at my inestimable, unguessable age, needs an extemporaneous work out. No senile servile flabby tabby's please.

Here's presuming, assuming you are foxfire fluorescent of the krypton Atomic number 9, counting the 8 extra lives, whiskery cats are fairy dragon fly gifted with. This curious metaphor, embodying the deftness of cat, fail safe landing on sticky gumshoe, padded shoes. Even if dropped head first, by some cowlick, knickers, pesky tester. I use this abstract idiom to illustrate, conjoin with my fate. For as of early and late, I am a travel case, layered with worn frayed lives, some more moth eaten than others. Here's Hesperus wishing, I carried a bar with assorted green blue brown little glass liquor bottles, to fix and mix, inside my cat case. Providential guided, provided with a gleaming key, to unlock the lock, open the flesh tummy drawer, in my glossy fluff blue pants, choose and pour. Purr at the bite.

I know, I know, your thousand corn ears are burning, popping popcorn, over the mewing news of myself as a suitcase, packed with covert suspended lives, costume folded inside. Bidding me to monkey return, with the riant organ grinder, grinding out the catchy tune, while I hoof and sing my song. But I need to overnight chill on the fatidic mystery, then Cheshire cat catch it, rat drag it to you.

Meanst while, I am too distracted by the wrack and turning screw wrath, of the covenant congregation's, moidore basket hoarder. Furtively lurking in the snow capped bushes, by the open, for late strays door; from the rafters it is raining fiery Hell and brimstone. The wailing non reverent reverend, offers no amen amends . Me thinks with a wink, he tips the silver chalice to his fish gulping lips, stained from swilling too much holy blood, draining the dregs. Bringing on the mean, Mr. Hyde side, the clumsy six tailed monster, that skunk possesses when one is drunk. Cat of nine tails preaching "O Safety pin your tongue to lip, so ye shall not be one with beasts!" (If the dispirited congregation, achieved this totality with cats, be they concord and celebrating.) O linked with the winking, small flesh full of heat and lightness. Pouncing batting, frisking leaves or whirling prismatic snowflakes, levity glissading, purring little tigers.

O Lord, keep me a ploucostomus, post humus vacuum lips sucking up debris, blind cave fish bottom dweller. O excuse me! No one can be a "bottom" dweller, x that text immediately, from arousing tempestuous temptations. The Old testament black bible, ballad of straight jacket laced superscribed inscriptions. Tattooed under the eyelids, in neon pink, to read rant chant in the dark. Puritanical prescriptions writ on flaming blood red scarlet letter A, letter head. Sent - via the lurching church, to a hack job, leech sucking, limb sawing doctor. In huddling cuddling cahoots with the reverend priests, to plug shut the ears with dripping searing wax. Sew up the nostril holes, and if the fading cat eye marbles, (as an owner of two global blue cat eyes, this analogy maketh the hair on my neck stand up straight) still see, vulture pluck them out, with a red hot fired up spoon.

Toxically over amphed, seduced by strung out nerves. The fiery preaching leader, shooting paranoia, streaming into their green veins. And O what a narcotic is paranoia. These "methamphetamine" heightened, demon enlightened devotees. Steered by shivering fears into vengeful witch hunters. Seeking seeing wolves with dagger grinning teeth, bristling in blind shadows. Beneath the umbrage of tree speaking trees, friends and neighbors "witnessed," offering up their glistening nakedness, to be joined with the horse loin, Goat horned Satan. Deceived by their nascent ears, filled with insidious lies, projecting eyes, the malign acolytes usurped of their star bone affinity with infinity. Primitively anthropomorphizing the Urania spheres. The floating pin cushion penetrating stars, like the pincushion dolls, the driven venomously sewed, embellished with spun gold, devil red, or black as the Black Sea, tresses Scissor cut while the victim shut her lids (in brief reprieve, maybe dream scape escaping, this contrived Devil's playground). The snipped hair sewn on the golliwog head, finger nail parings, stuck on the cloth target pointing finger tips, pieces of dresses worn, pages contaminated with the victims' prints, stitched onto the eery doll. Sticking knitting needles through the cottony space, where the flesh doppelgangers' sinewy heart, is hard wired to thump. To halt or sicken, the jump roping, blood pumping muscle stricken. These ranting Mephistopheles, seeing the steely cold eyes of stars, as pin head pricking Satan's piercing stares. The muscles in their clam shells fluttering shuddering, at their own unconscionable savagery.

Another skunky pet peeve of mine, the pet slogan: "Cleanliness is next to Godliness" embroidery framed on malaise walls. Appearing to lack any affluence of influence. Instead of the catchy abstraction. The actual act of studying salubrious cats would teach the bathed and sanitary hygiene meanings. Inspiring aspiring believers to worship cats, like Nile river engineering

Egyptians. Piling offerings of fish, bowls of delish thick dyspepsia cream, at our catnip scratching post, Demi god altars. Vigorous and vigilant enemies of louse. Dirt mean quadruped ambassadors of Mr. Clean. Rough nitty gritty scrubbing tongues, gussy up cleaning machines. Rubbing out any flake fleck mote speck, of a Lady Macbeth guilt ridden spot. Our persimmon, gray haze, tricolor calico, zebra stripey, blue, clan pristine. Whether we be rooted in the double humped water cisterns camel blinking sands, the monkey bread baobob twisting trees, of the jaguar jungle patterned, equinotical green juiced tropic, or the fish stinking streets of this roller coasting coast. The dazzling cat synagogue, agog! Polishing, abolishing dirt, with elbow grease and sanding tongue fervor. The little tiger tellurium workers, gag on hair balls, wearing the efflorescent stripe of glossy duty.

As for the inbred dibble and dabble, sit in the grungy tub, after five bakers rub a dub, germinating germs, duped villagers, Get a grip on it! Half witted partisans, squatting on a splinter ranked plank, with a donut hole in the middle. Hiding behinds, behind, an oblivious infant moon, crib carved on the shabby door decor. Disease brewing breeders. Grunting while producing, infectious piles and piles of swamp high shit. Their pollution solution; henchmen digging trenches, delivering waste into the incurable, turbid moaning, patient river.

Entailing another de tailed (ouch!) tale. Paws tip toeing silently, like the moccasin feet of squaws, sensing the nature veiled beckoning, feline dig a hole. Poop, tails held banner high. Leaves, green toilette wipes. Then civil business finished, with diligence, rake over the deposit, erased, leaving no trace. When was the last time your ear wells, gondola channeled, swelled with the malignant news, of a cat with cholera?

To our zodiacal chronicled youth, we cats display, for art's sake, the paw ladling of nervous eye fish. Also scout ferreting out, strapping rats and corn fed bloated mice for lunch. Munching on crispy cock roach critters scuttling afoot, when the pickings are slim Jim, for a providential sent essential protein. Our tailing young, osmosis, under the skin, take it all in. Chess game gain, from the live demonstration. Besides "navy seal" training, to stave off the cloak and dagger stabbing pain, of creeping hunger.

We resolutely salute the tempering of tempers. Honor the Whoa! Pulling back the stampeding horse, showmanship curving the impetuous, prompting the entente. Hampering paws from clawing at the Adam's apple jammed in the trachea blocked, choking on chunks of biblical junk, converts. It is a challenge not to crouch and leap, swiping with our jaguar cousins' mentor paw precision, at jugulars, frustrated beyond belief, relief. To affront confront these aping gaping, uniformed conformed followers to think, see straight through the hazing. Still it is the ignorant who bear the shame of bullet fueled feuds, the vigilante hangings, of undefended impetuously judged, dangling corpses. Blind folding conscripted weapon sanctioned children, into scattering the dice of bones wars.

Cat spats (shrieking yowling growling, swatting paws, biting ears, but not lethal by a long stretch). The short fused dispute, usually provoked stoked over witch bewitched Tom cat, master of Tom foolery. Ushers, the blushing, blue star tiara, tiger lily fragrant, star gazing, suggestively raised tail, female. Strutting her fateful Phoebe stuff, beneath the regal sphinx moon.

But binding joys and desires, to inhale repentance smoking incense? Bats in their belfries! Say I, one of the Devil's, small furred cranial furnaces. My stiff, non flex, though twitching when annoyed, (a nervous cat's Turrets), witch in this reprobate, window peeking. Turn of the screw, witch navigating, depressive aphelion , pick who you envy, hate, paranoid ungated, approbate zone. Surrounded by the jealous zealous, only have intercourse through a hole cut in the sheet, with body's covered, like they are damn Ku Klux Clan crazed ghosts, my disavowed tail tics more often than not.

Yet that is later, the dunce hatted K.K.K., white supremacy members hiding beneath, bleached whiter than white sheets. And as alluvion alluded to earlier, more or less. I have ingested, eternity's blinking stars, time release capsule. Though spasmodically encapsulated, Big Dipper dipped, into non sequential sequined sequences. Possessed by endless, cloaked, furtive furry lives. Wearing the same bona fide, but dragon reactivated, cat whisker costume. I first blind kitten opened my eyes in, to earn learn Ozium prism vision. Though my exposed psyche, changing a thousand fold with Thyme seasoned reasoning. The mercurial agility of youth, re-amping, re-inhabiting my golden bones. Cargo dispatched on the new outer limits, of a jaguar shaking quaking jungle. Whether resurrected, along with the stadium walls of a crumbled past, or futuristic cement jungle, sky rumbling with glinting dragon tail wind whipping mono rails. Transported through the channeling portal, to gladiator dark ages before, or light years zapping tapping into the vacillating, snow globe sprinkling unknown .

Tend I then, to rely on the Dog Star's guiding tail. To point out witch Ursa Minor thunder struck bellowing roaring century I was in, when who was accused, hung, beheaded. Witch holy war was four horses of the Apocalypse, Urania bidden, driven from the pearly stables, dashing out of the pearl jam, spermous star spheres, prophesy spurred, lured to earth. Delivering the Gabriel horned message, of their prophetic apparition, to the avenging warriors. The whites of the terrestrial horses, terrified eyes glowing, as the mounted theroids (who never asked to bear the steroid wrathful, iron fisted, strangling reined riders) fell to their knees. Bleeding like Saint Sebastian, hung upside down from a thick branched tree, shot full of arrows. The guileless horses praying for the bugling red masked death, to thrall release each glossy equestrian soul. Tenderly folding it in his scarlet robes, returning it to the capering turquoise fields, of early amber colt green apple days. O Beausefulus, enslaved by bridle whip and bit, prisoner forced coerced, into a decorated war horse.

Yes, be I a bit pessimistic, but the salty black blooded histories, of Ides of March plunging swords, bubonic flea biting plagues. Ring around the Rosie, black posy impose on my premature, mellifluous mellow geniality. Black perambulator wheeled, to a leaner meaner demeanor, boneless shadow curtained carriage. For alas, one cannot paralyze the ganglion mass, to stifle the rising empathy, and the "your pain is my pain" exchange, throws off one's tympanum balance. Tented by the doldrums of this gone weak in the knees, shaky, peeled onion teary hold, one can lose one's footing, fall off the fence. Hence end up a sniveling basket case.

What is it, that old saying? "Pride goeth before a fall." For the Cat woman Bast's, Lesbos Bosom sake! My intestines tied in knots, equilibrium spinning, my dandy dapper galvanizing sense of satyriasis, forsakes, escapes, inflates me. But one must twist the buttons through the button holes again, casually itch behind an ear, dust off the bottom of one's silky britches, and march on. Purring hissing twisting, leathery licorice lips into a flirtatious smile. Puffing out manly little chest, with moxie conviction, magnetizing, advertising to the star dusted lunar lion heart ladies. As it is their catnip capering, coy open invitation, flickering sapphire blue fire desire, that keeps my slick, smooth licked fur, glossy.

In truth, rather than puncturing lungs with tiger incisors, and gauntlet ripping the still beating hearts out of bone crushed vests, to Saturn devour. Puss and Boots Lance Alot sword clashing, lashing, about in plum purple ostrich plume tickling hat. Matching vest, chaps, suede knee high,silver mouse charm jingling, from bold zipper boots. Savage purple liberating, distressed, dangling in snarling slobbery jaws, fading fainting, damsels. Mistress saved, in my hairy manly cat arms. Looting from farmers slave possessing, bronze or golden, halcyon cows. Squirting milk from utterly pink swollen utters, into shining knight pails. Robin Good inviting, muffy ear hatted, yearning mamma and kits, to an over the pale milk bar.

Though that wood cut, a persuasive, purple theater draped caped, thrilling daredevil hero. I purringly prefer to be a pondering pacifist. Keening my claws, on the bark of a screaming tree. O dear, that so did not come out right! A little tiger of Lilith, dwelling in the rainbow wreathed garden of limbo, included as one of the coveted Peaceful Kingdom. Twilight blue lambent Lilith, fife piping her silver tongued, fluid migration into sleep, melodious melodies. Across the Lotus eater ripening, ice cream white petals, fugue mood gardens. Ribbons lovingly tied in swishing manes, green rippling fur. Creatures sleeping, paws hooves fins curled beneath their coruscating shape.

Yeah, as they disintegrate, green dandelion fluff falling out, covering the dead leaf floor. Jelly eyes melting in the sockets, bald piano bones strewn across the garden abstract.

Ah! Lilith, the first born unicorn woman, expelled from Eden for her ardent prism hearts, growing on blue vine veins, beneath her evening stirring flesh. Sister to the splashing vermeil fire bird wings, Lucifer. Closed wings flung, exiled from Cloud 9, for his uncompromising saintly beauty. An eyesore, for the jealous unknown, still born God.

Like that rainbow wreathed, sweet pea garden, would ever bequeath its shade, invite me to taste its tasty verdant speared grasses. anyway---

(Sorry, for the split forked wriggling diversion of my unrepenting serpent tongue. But I do so love to put the unhatched T.V. screen, of this grim dim beggar stumped world, on pause. Paw pushing the remote mute button, to sloping neck, one legged crane zen. Thousand golden sky wings dipped sun sanguine, sampan crimson sail, dream stream beyond). The somber subdued, static electricity shades of gray Reality T.V. here in Saturnine shanty town. Where television is light years from its signaling radio waves, incunabola boob tube birth. Electricity lightening rods, antenna jawing radio waves, dispatched from tinny boxes, with tuning in nubs, do not chatterbox host the coast yet. Let alone satellites, to spoon feed us whatever dish we wish. What a black out, save for the stray electricity sparks, bouncing off our pouncing, sensitized violin string whiskery, whisking wind whistling, little tiger sprinting fur.

When its not the preacher blasting, apocalyptic, frugal Spartan, locked chastity belt, rigamortis winter. For who would nakedly unite in this trumping zero zero? Witch mirror glass bewitches most of the yearling year (excepting of course, lively Bast cats). Though we fur people can still rag time, entwine, spooning wind. Yin Yang swivel, swizzle, dusted by florid frozen flakes and stellar dust, in our green heat, melting freeze. So wearing snow roses, flake woven bridal trains, we sensually gyrate generate, celestial share, even in bare winter.

But when the elements invite, do I love to sand dust, rolling down dunes, in my thinner springy coat. Out and about cat fish loping, aroma roam esplanades, where tiny sand crabs pincer pinch a zingy tickle. As the foam frolicking sea, is not far from a watchful band of cat callers, cat- erwauling warnings. In the splurging spree, free spirit of spring, I plant wending paw prints in the starfish glowing sand, that the rakish radical wind, anarchist ally erases. Just in case I am witch chased or hunted. I, whose espionage wire whiskered ears, hear the blue haired, turquoise skin, flipping dolphin tail mermaids. Siren singing, ringing across the undulating, undinal cat's cradle rocking sea. Joyously estranged, from the bed post headed, strange Bible thumping, corn husk blank doll face, pin cushion throbbing needle doll town, that so gives me the heebie jeebies!

How we each of us need our lamb safe port, resort from the storm. Where one can scribble Save Me! On messages scroll rolled, tapped into green glass swan neck bottles, flung far into the purple manteau, lost horizon. Bravely bottle bobbing in and under the swirling face, of the rhythmic pulsing, raging liquid lion sea. Argosy arriving, on the kitty litter gritty shores, of some vacated, carapace lovingly piled on carapace, paradisal sanctuary. Reliquary treasure island elevating, from the moody acrobatic sea, to deliverance, beneath the flaming flamingo pink anchorite sun. Oh purr! Please allow me to tune out here, catching a few heavenly winks. Drifting in and out, of this stoking, cat arm stroking, mirage. Lashless lids, slits shut tight. A quick catnap, snooze marooned on the heated maroon beach. A crème de menthe, nite cap extreme foam please!

You come too!

Ahhhh! A slinky stretch, springs rewound to Leap year leap. Now where were we? Me? Just let me paw flick the sand witch from my eyes—That's better.

Back to my Cynosure woofing constellation revelation. Wish it was Felix the cat, reliably tail ticking time, pointing to witch juxtaposed, plague contagious age, cyclic season, of my spiracle spouting, codified references I am referring to. Codified. Excuse me while I Ugh! Yuck! Hiss spit and retch. Good riddance, rid myself of that nasty base taste. Codified, ear well tintinnuabulating clinging, ringing of cod liver oil! Worm hooks, fishes up from the glassy castle blue refracting pool, of the memory. A Tudor amber hair braided in ropes, proclivity filled with good will, little maiden. Her hazel eyes deep as fiords. She, a golden pear held high in the driad tree's barren leaf bare arms. Rhapsodically glimmering gilded gold, against a color thieved, beaten lamb eaten winter. Yet I feel it in my fossil old bones, that the holes in the leaking cabbage soup heads,of these superstition driven folks, descry eye her hair as Devil red. Ignoring the community's commonality, with her pallid complexion. This snake charming She, who was pirated here, on a scurvy sea sick puking ship. Nadir neir, north of any where, must be better than here. This Golgotha, skulls and bones piled around the Godless execution charred grounds. This dying swan town, where ashen, soldier of the Lord mothers, bake powdery Christian animal crackers, with crosses over their eyes, as guerdons, for their urchin trained crusaders.

For shame! I must bite off my tongue, stung with spite, for not exorcist exercising, corsetted discretion. In examining the far or near sighted pages of, cat stretching contrary ages, nary appearing to be Northern Lights, Aurora Borealis illuminated. I who have been launched, by the steel toe boot of the brute future, swastika barb wire "ethnic cleansing" Nazis. Witnessed the screaming bombings of maimed nameless beggar children, and shelter seeking bleeding felines, in the Middle East masked mosque streets.

Staggeringly beheld the infamous "Little Boy" atomic plutonic mushrooming leukemia plagued cloud, dispersing nefarious vapors. Where bald featherless, seared seraphs, with blood dripping tears, humanely wept over hurriedly shoveled mass graves, at the end of the suicide, genocide, sterile world.

But let us stray cat away from these camps, of requiem lamentation, brutal degradation, tattooed starvation. Keeping the melting faces, toxic visage traces, of exiled races, cache stashed in a gap under my spinal cord. For if I paw step risking the way, over this poison soupy brewing, bubbling bog, the quicksand beneath will surely yank a half pint, (wish I could swig a nip) like myself, (though I am a fat cat of mine own, whiskery mythical, Even at Odds, making), beneath the sucking suffocating muck. Glug Glug! Glug! Doomed to review the same Kodak living color, three dimensional memory photos, over and over, even when propelled into other dimensions. Viewing the dragging feet, tragic danse macbre, until I am so broken, the pieces will not fit.

Before I habitually interrupted myself, I was purple pig rooting about for truffles, to infuse introduce the strawberry sweet girl. This dainty levin lass, soars beyond the barbed wire limits, transcending the spotted cow emulsion. Who gag me with a spoon fed me the vile cod liver oil.

During the throes of a distemper sickly state of hissing clawing madness, after some nasty little Johnny Ding Dong bell, pushed me in a hell bottomed well. She charitably dragged me out, with winters freezing blue fingers, choking my throat. Teeth clattering chattering, soaked to the bone in that Golem's stone cold tomb home. Trial and error patiently, she heave hoed me up, up in the rope strung sneezing water bucket. After being swaddled in towels, massage licked by the hearth's fervent tongues, mother love, furnace fueled. I recovered my fishy wits, and she put the fat back into the cat. Sibylline, vivisection diagnosing, by tuning fork tuning into the body's humming locution.

A real Lilith healer, saving old Lazarus for this Haley's comet, showering over the stern town houses, swarthy panther night, rubbing its fur against the panes.

Why the nimbus encompassing her summer vixen hair, gold as a gold finch. Want I to paw inch within, purring motor furred car, circumference of her. Not that cars puff and cough about the crooked nose streets yet. But this rhyming Queen Mab, married to the man in the moon's dark side. The glittering icy rings of Saturn, her engagement rings. And her unicorn horned rocking horse, has broken loose, from the ball and chained gravity rockers. U.F.O. levitating to the ceiling, then down down to the wooden floor, he roars and nursery clatters across.

While outside, hidden in the snow dressed greenery, hungry red predatory peering eyes, searing smoking nostrils, press to the glass. The pack carousing, bristling hyenas. A local patrol of hoofed witch hunters, in this Deuteronomy, Old Testament revered bibles, stacked to the moon, make me swoon with dread, undefended bodies, burned to swirling ash, hamlet. Though their gibbet eyes can see, they prickling scent sense, the ponied instrument of the Devil. The church pack panting to piss, on the pony's Stonehenge inherent magic. The roaming hoofed pack, foaming at the mouth, waiting for the sign, to rabidly attack, cannibalize the pagan horned pony. And the raven clever, Devil red haired girl, arcanely named "Sirroco," for a fervent sent southerly wind. Who rhythmically rides the narwhale horned unicorn. Gliding beyond this print toasting, scorched pages fluttering, burning of learned books. Ignited incited by banshee screeching ignorance. Sirroco, with a natural affinity for science, who writes with her left hand. Must me thinks, learn to mirror reflect, Leonardo write backwards in her anatomy illustrated note books.

Who aureate laureate doctored me, led me to sainted stasis. Nourished me (I am not referring to that frog's breath tasting, whisker straightening, corpse raising, cod liver oil!) Although she artfully administered the hideous but healing medicine, in loving spoonfuls. I near by here by pledge to watch dog, safeguard, shield this rare green deer, by Lion ripping out the throats, of the whole pin cushion stabbing army, if needs be. And yes, accepting as truth, the pharos luminosity of alchemy. Fated, written in the stars, gifted to those touched by recondite talents.

As for these hare flitting witted, mustard grass scansions, of elapsed collapsed ages, crossing my eyes, like a cat that needs corrective lenses. (I would not in the least object, if I could get my paws on say, some dusky blue or purple contacts from the swinging 21st century. But talk about the call to censor, the heavy stockade frames, and window thick pane pains, clumsily modeled in witch burning Massachusetts—Forget it! I'd even with poise and aplomb, Siamese feline wear my crossed eyes instead. Pre purring prefurring to be visually impaired, who is most usually dazed anyway, in a sequentially mixed ages, amazed maze. Walking on eggs across the frosted world's wedding. Where warm bedding is sparse as a smile.

Of course, off course, for my eggs are scrambled. As they, (the timed periods out of line) tango together like a school of salty red herrings, tail dancing on the slapping surface of the sunken vessels, treasure seizing sea.

Sibilance confessing, I deserve to be ruse confused. As the bombastic fall out, for relying on the cipher component of dog. Even a sky trucking trafficking, mystic navigating, star studded, crepuscular eyed, Siberian of the North. Majorly, Ursa Minor's. For Cats, on the other hand, or independent signing paw, proponent propend, instinctively defend tidiness. Pink salmon wreathed with locus focus, librarian filing automatic systematic order. Dogs, bounding out of bound, leaping, rolling into the stench of decaying seals, or the smellier the better, feces of any species. Tracking excrement and mud all over the rug Ugh! O for the lissome license of cat! Can those slobbery sporadic, fawning doggy beasts, even read?

Now, if the shoe were on the other foot, (sorry for the tired, old school shoe beaten, elves and shoemaker, locution execution). And the holy Bast apotheosis ascended, in this steering wheel Meowing, North Star symbiotic, open skylight, navigational, Felix ticking tail, blue star outlined transitional position. You can bet your claws, or toe nails, (watch they aren't swiped off the floor, we have discussed those needle doll nail paring, blaring consequences before) for the incarnate barely haired species. She O queen of Queens, (x nay on Brooklyn bridge vicinity Queens, is altogether untethered, not dome bone cracked, or even rooster routed, to salt and peppery hen's, revolving ovary eggs. Let alone, Holy pedagogic mother of pecking peeping order Hen, roosting on the pedigreed impeccable golden egg, O dream of Queens). Bast, O Cleopatra of cats, her indelible royal highness, capped mapped with shining dignity and wit. Tail compass pointing, to witch Pompeii swallowed east was west, for her lost, whiskered and straggly bearded fishy breath, albatross crossed, squid inked, "Alas the sea is as stained as we" sailors. Bast masted, devil fish gliding argosy, riding the tempestuous liquid lion sea. Naturally, for her own preferred fur, chromosomes linked like beads into necklaces, persnickety yowling cousin, witch bewitched age was sage.

By the why, hereby spelled out, a design behind the chaffing of rascallion canines. The intrigue I cannot seem to flea myself of, ever since a clamped jaw attack by an unprovoked, minotaur fierce pit bull. The raging (testosterone sacks in tact) bull, refused to eject, until I swiped its tender rose nose. Punctured and bleeding, a crimson sprinkler, spread eagled, winded, finally crutch dragging my anemic self to higher grounds. Traumatized by the knock at the scarlet robed skeleton, hammering its xylophone bone horse, behind a bloated Gothic gargoyle, slumped in sleep, sated on its fat intake of blood. Door left open wide, for any toe stumped cherub to see. This grotesque but intimate enough encounter, gifting me with post traumatic stress. Hence ever since developing a zero tolerance for dogs.

And my carking, nagging, furnace venting, about the minus of, a systematized mode of decoding interloping passageways, on the intermingling interminable turnpike, of my drenched cat revived lives, triggers my hairline temper. My intertidal shilly shallying, splashing (though I have mastered a muscular cat crawl, if I may say so myself!) Medley of mixed bag, unaligned pieces and missing puzzle parts, I must Jonah swallow, gives me hick ups! Hissy fits! O I do so fear the nin nothingness, just floundering in a black sea, a surcease of zombies, floating up from the sunken ship, bottomless bottom. Sea weed, anchor wrapped about ankles, slithering, stretching, snapping, torn fibrous shackles, freeing the bulging eye ghoulish ghouls.

As for the spectacle(s) I do believe I am in need, of the flapping cuckoo tongued, sloppy rag tag, drunk tank dunking dog paddle. No hold your tail high, stream lined feline, would ever be seen in such a slap stick, laughing stock, looking glass, distorting carnival mirror. Dogs are clowns, jesters, knaves, can't even clean egg off their face, to save face. But yes, I guess this is part of their endearing child like charm. Loyal red badge loyalty, defending the master until death, and in ghostly after hours after wards. Cats, the master of their own sampan, shirt sail, tail gale flapping, pumpkin orange striped tail, fish slapping, leap frog leaping destiny.

Besides staying afloat in these tides, ides of March wavelengths. I do hate swimming, or worse, slipping into a portal holed toilet, particularly of an out house. Why the thought of it gives me wet feet. Achoo! My telltale tail, flicks on the switch, to the nervous tick twitch. As far as bathing in the claw footed European tub,(who are they trying to kid, invite, by identifying with the claws? At least ponds and seas, eager receivers of open lid pickle barrels, dumped full of fat silver coin fish to seize. My mitten mitts, smitten with smite, to bite off the head of a bumper sticker, Jesus cross in the blank eyes, fish. So much for my four footed, seven toe fisted pacifist claim. Be we all burdened with incorrigible hunger pangs, which rip tooth shark, sharpen our fangs. And there are no Jesus fish bumper stickers, or cars so far, as I de tailed before, in this drab current dragging life. Only crack the whip! hay paid slave horses, carting the tightly religious corseted convicts,who pay, pray to simply inhale,exhale free air. The iron irony of their pitiful, unmerciful peasant burlap bagged, sacked, boot licking, lacky subservience. To a papal throned usurping demagogue, or minstrel ministry, disturbia disturbing. Strikes a lightening striking comradery, with the Peter Breughel realist surrealist painting of "The Blind Leading the Blind." Witch scare summons, from the cellar stables, the pregnant white lightening blinding night mares. Knocking down doors, with their glinting atomic nightmare shoes. Has the door in the corridor, leading to Peter Breughel, even been unlocked, turned, twisted open yet? " O dear, I do get so muffled, wooly brained, trying to sort out witch stitch to drop, or pick up, to darn the darn needle yarned muffler, holding Today's wind at bay. Sometimes I could just walk the plank, jump, under tow ankle yanked, succored by the lonely old man, who shuffles across the sandy blue sand dollar bank. Beneath the tyrannical Titan Triton's, angry fork pronged sea.

Like that would be solvent, with me fated to be sucked into an oceanic gaping stalactite cave mouth. Spiracle spewed, vomited forth into the tributary fingers of some nearby mucky river. Ugh! Brr! Flushed, stuffed into a turbid rusty broken pipeline, gushed, regurgitated into another new moon, dragging her fetal birth sack, like a poisonous jelly fish, epoch era.

O well then, old chap, milky chin up, suck it all in. Imagine the burden on Grandfather Twilight's' tick tock clock yoked shoulders. There since the beginning of no beginning! Wending his Gemini, nacre shoe footing, across each teaser and the fire cat, tabbying dimension, is beyond comprehension! My hat's off to the billion fold old birthday boy! Born under the illusion of older then old, wise and wizened, spindrift spuming hair, cloud drift beard. Weird, his skipping rope pace never phased. The passing of dates, just deepens the bolting cobalt in his green emanating spring eyes.

As for this teeter tottering back and forth, balloon blowing into the next yawning mouth, saurian smiling, ravenous razor teeth lacuna. I blame it on Einstein. After all, he Is the guy who pussy foot trespassed, cat harassed, moused it all up. For what you prove can happen, happens. Happenstance is lanced, after being hooked, dragged up from the Nirvana sea weed temple, secret swirling, bottom of the sea. Or by dialing the indigenous, hurdling through outer space, red telephone booth, it answers. (He won't much feel at home in these ash dusted, staked out, whipping boy tied to the fire licking, roasting tender loin stake.)

Make no mistake, his anarchistic creativity, frames him as a striking red deer target! Even as his ubiquitous, unrestrained meditative presence does. Why in his last moon kitten, back water flushing rushing through the rippling pink brain cavern; where naked Leda feathers by, on a great blue cygnet trumpeting swan. This, the pithy androgynous pit, processional processing of his tune in drop out, naked ingenious genus genesis. Miraculously encapsulated within his infant crawling, pulling himself to standing, to pedaling a red three wheeler velocipede. Proceeding feeding into two tires idle wheel spinning, meditating on the speed of light years. The reflecting dazzle from a dead star, whose vital rays just galvanized us. Knickers for the little dude with infinity whirling within his spirited spheres. The conforming German Teachers (sadly militant usurping!) referring to Route 66 standards, detected projected the kindergarten through 8th grade Albert, mentally deficient. Fortunately, their circumsional disquisition did not "What the Lord giveth he taketh away" convince the distant little whiz. But if he even listened to those censuring, hammer head pounding critics. The blessed, obsessed detective scientist, rocket glistening, stellar dusted child; turned a blind ear to their lip service. So crowned is this wizard, with stellar cat curiosity. Wait until he steps out of the bubble, skirting beneath the prism whiskered star, meets these green face scowling crooked nose witch hunters!

Though I do not wish my self generating percolating colleague, to jutting nose Plymouth Rock arrive, any where near this base, promontory base, erased bus station. I forgive him (though do bear a slight short sighted resentment), for my whiskers dipped in eternity's light, plight.) The odd, sticking out his tongue, whirling white maelstrom of hair (I could give that fountain head a good licking! Why doth he not useth his own proud tongue he sticks out, for the world to catch in photographs) for the simple act of grooming? Eh? Though the closets filled with cloned suits, shoes, shirts, ties man, is like one of my cat clan Bask family members. A first rate five star mate, when we find ourselves together, canon balling, comet shooting backwards or forwards, whizzing past the turret fossil ears, of the interminable Grandfather Twilight. Albert likes to stroke and stroke forgetfully, behind my blue velvet pyramid ears, under my milky way swirling chin, with his enormous globular black eyes staring off. Star gazing beyond, a universe encompassing a universe, encompassing a universe... His intricately, nimble cat balanced, mathematically proven time travel theory, embraced as absolute proof in the flaming Holiday pudding. Dead on hypothesis, thesis, witness authenticated, by the both of us. Who don't know the underground tubular garden feeding, sleeping, oblivious burial grounds of death, and Lazarus rise, sliding past nimbus absolution, absolved of any sin. Chuckle hiss hairball retch! I resort retort with hare lipped, nibbling sarcasm, about the incubus succubus sucking, leeching drain of Biblical ordained sins. But tragically, the transcript conscript scriptures, can Judas grip, cripple twist, boulder on shoulders, flatten a disciple.

Yet the ambient lambent and stroking kindness, of my furnace stoking little tiger, fur purring religion, humming bird whirs for itself. Our Egyptian palm frond fanned, grand dam, pyramid stellar, cellar preserved, cat mother of mothers, Bast... Divinely lithe, of lovely trim waist and slim limb, posed in jewel naval exposed, fish bone earrings and necklace, violet transparent pantaloons, and halter riveting top. Cleopatra, gray girl decked out on the cobalt smooth, jewel ornamented, solar heated love seat... Endears herself to worshipers by slipping stripping out of her mummy wrappings, with delta ray precision. Jack in the box pops open her revered sarcophagus, (adorned with swiveling Yin Yang wrapped cats, kissed by shimmering moon lips) every mournful minute a feline child's fur flies and he dies. Rendered limp, bundles him against her hosanna homage fervency, until he is fervent sun Bast basking against her purring heat. Swaddled in her indelible essence presence, and is ready to give up the ghost. But his spirited kai, the Ariel spirit, makes a transparent wing, buzzing bee line, back to the returning hallowed cats' sphinx guarded tomb. Manically, panically, given the strength of a thousand little tigers, (as he is no demi god or deity) muscles open her sarcophagus. The intriguing lid, painted in her seductive, leaping fish, esoteric Lorelei soprano siren singing, golden slinking beneath the anchorite sun anointed image. His holy kit ghost, digs under her now wrapped and re wrapped like Christmas packages, bandages, crawling into her nutmeg sprinkled womb. Packed in like sardines, with the other invisibles, though they take up no space. (How many angels can dance on the head of a pin? How many cat ghosts can flutter in Bast's mystic womb, holding station tomb?) Until the red phone booth, hurdling through space, rings the appointee up. He answers, the supreme call of duty, kai slipping back back into the waiting fetal birth sack. Swimming towards the opening tunnel, engaging his head, he slips through. Blind for a few days a weak, umbilical anew kitten. So, the questing question: do any of us, totally resolve, dissolve ourselves, with no revolving door returns. RIP forever, in the pearly midnight trembling, petal pleated, dusky enfolding, puckered shut, spear fence, gate closed, for late night repose, garden?

Okay compadre, we have crossed over many light fluxing flexing bridges together. Myself harping, not delicately plucking the arched imperial pearly gate instrument. Tickled by gilded tresses, always returned to the blush of youth, lepidoptera winged, Seraphs; with nirvana vibrating, tear dripping strings. (Aged sunken cheek, wrinkled angels never modeled, must be stabled somewhere, or closet locked?) But rude dog barking during most of the straying, levin seeking, yet weighing complaints. You, still in patient shadow pursuit of my sundering sickle sweeping, thundering, sore tendons, melancholic, tine, tinder box, sparked, fluctuating candle manifestation. So without more cavil rattling, bring to you, in traditional Bastian grace (even bowing kow towing, to the about to be a fur orderb, but dallied with, hung onto by the tail strand mouse. Whether he is king queen or pauper, regardless of his piddling or regal ranking order.)

The pointed stricture self afforded, I will take in biding stride. Immersing in the galvanization, edification on my dilatory display of manners. Miss Manners atonement for my lagging waggery. Resort to better use of perfuse conduct, ushered in to fluff the cat, so to speak. So without further flinging the quills, evasive hedgehog hedging "How do you do," and all that copacetic jazz, as I extend my favored fore paw to you, in solitary salutation. The appellation, that fits my fur coat vibration, is Lazarus. Now, if that does not suit, as moon flower armor over the fish's guts. I don't know what could "kick the can" to the moon better. And yes, it is all about hide and seek, amid these Salem ugh! Water dunking, if she floats she's a witch, if she sinks, she's just dead, trialing trials. The high light of these God fearing, for God would slap them down with his big wig mitts, like annoying mosquitoes, if He lived (within ear, mosquito buzzing distance of them).

Now that's a fumbling stumbling in the dark intrigue, I've never laid eyes on. Can't say I want to. The way He spits out skulls and cross bones, splits wish bones, piling them up on the sides of his carved human flesh, dinner plate, its worse than The Dark Ages!

Leaping jack rabbits back, not to the waxy ventriloquist frozen smile angels, I beg you on my flexion knees, please! Any night of the year, I'll take the humane, human like angels, weeping blood tears, at the brink of the smoky flying ash world,

But creeping back to stalking my catfish sphere eyed stalking horse, concealing fears, talking shadow, intimate silhouette. Equipped with my disoriented, Artful Dodger, jay bird jabbering persona...Meow me you, kindling our relationship. I do so hope, after granting the official (though invisible) indivisible paw shake. We feel a five armed, phosphorous sea star seal, of intimate converse, a ghostly symbiosis, in the absence of the sweet meat of form. (A swelling though silent sonic welcome, if you be a tourist from any looming beyond galaxy.) Just as long as you are not part of the fanatic posse. One of the torching, witch hallucinating, hologram jammed, water multiplying lobster red devils everywhere, including your holy lineaments underwear. Howling lupine moon, above the trembling pines, accursed murderous half dead's! In witch dire case, I would be a water witch floater, in your Gothic mind's eye. In grave, needle in the eye, pinhead cat doll, fire danger! Yet through the invisible, I whisker sense, vermeil bonds of sanctioned conviviality, hence, tying us together. So onwards and upwards we go, toe to toe.

Again in describing my inimitable (except by my evil twin. Prey he's not harvesting, a surfeit of evil genius kits!) In touring the contour of my fur bone presence, as wearing the most debonair flaring white gloves, two pairs on the 7 hang loose toes of each handy foot. The gloves hiking up my stylish ankles, turned to silk socks. Dressed to kill, (borrowing an untimely double ontondo from the future), as a blue tuxedo cat. Though tuxedos have not been silk emperor, imperial worm precision vision sewn yet, threaded by countless thread thin fingers. In pink salmon, spring green salamander hiding, solstice lingering lack of chromatic shades, Salem. Not by these, lock the sinner in stockades, swallow the skeleton key. If she cures someone, quick, block her in, hunt her down, drown her, she's a finger itching witch.

You may invest an interest in, the following mad cap clip. (Until now, it abominable snowman, melted from my mind). Translated from the buzzing drift, of our green eyed fly, spy on the wall. Busy transcendental transparent winged, sanctioned Vatican scansion. Ear antennae, moon eyes sanctioned, espionage hunting, golden paw tipped, detecting detectives. Feline reporting news to muse about. That the gun toting pope, web secreting, secretly spinning, hyped fiction friction, generated with benediction, the purgatorial incineration, of the accused. So any bewitching, dimpled, rose mouth pretty one, that a wagging tongue jealously views, rocketing on a broom, will vigilant vigilante do. (I hope that pope resides, in Dante's many layers, tortuous compartments, apartments of damnation!) The acumen instrument of God, waving the cape to annihilate, those who adagio dance with death. By daring to be born, not breech stuck inside, the blind cave, sewed up tight, vagina.

The Holy Grail wine, peppered with rakish papish spells, blind worm stings and poison forked tongues.

The webbing on these tutored revelations, too fragile to bridge across the fiords yet. Waiting for future reference, acceptance, because they always kill the messenger. Ex caliber sword in the stone stored, in the cerebral cortex, frontal lobes, beneath our cat hats.

Myself a harboring master, harbinger of this hazardous testimonial. Pharos positioning me, with Felix the Cat, (the a-fore-said wall icon in later centuries). Ticking off each penal minute, with his tail streamed efficient clock instrument. My ticked off turrets syndrome, symptomatic activated tail, seconding seconds, aligned with that black and white gloved cat. (Though I am minus his bottomless bag of tricks, witch I am surely sorely in need of. During this perennial thorn stabbing, season of the witch!) Renowned for its family gathering, theater of the grotesque. Containing, the entertaining gibbet, danse macabre, of noose strung, hung blue corpses. Swaying, feet one shoe dancing on the theology drama stage. The other matching brother, hollow shoe, hanging tongue dropped to the shocked ground below. Brought to you by, the signature hand, of the rope supplying pope. Myself, a small sparrow of Bast, quite helpless to cool the nefarious, bubbling boiling crucible. But my conscientious tail conscience, detailing every condemned act, motor speared into high gear. Its nervous tick propelled, assailed into frantic panic.

At that, tails are quite tactless instruments, emotional acolytes, with impetus lives of their own. A coded Rosetta stone key, in deciphering, the salient language of cats. Even if an indigo purring, claws retracted, legs rubbing feline, appears saccharine sweet, to craftily beg a treat. The twitching tail is the telltale, despite the kissy up performance.

Momentarily, releasing its pride, the lion providing pride, of its jungle drumming incunabula. The blushing cat disgusted at the treaty trade off. The scaled tail flopping from an apron pocket, wish of fish, having won the drooling little fiend over. But a puffed up Blow fish ego, is not worth the bag of bones, stripped of meat, by the needle teeth of savage starved piranhas.

Now where o where was I, mesmerized hypnotized by my curious butterfly eyes (by the while, curiosity did not kill the cat, it gifted kitty with cognizance). O yes-lucid spring water mirroring, my own furry bone, pyramid ear walking home, so you can envision my tail residence, more completely. Maybe piece by piece, puzzle fit together, my picture identity. Thus nodding to me, on the winter friendless fiendish, hail reigning streets. Stop to chew the fat, at that, invite me to sleep over, by the beckoning phantom feverish arms, of your welcoming hearth. Apprenticing me, to cat carry your slippers, read reckoning books to you. Such as: Kafka, Tolstoy, Chekhov, Lorca, Neruda too. If their creative legacies, have not been dispatched, sorceress printed yet. I hungry stranger cross the threshold, bearing gifts. My trusty attache case, carrying copies from other lingering integers. The page energized perduring pharos illuminated minds of artists. Galvanizing the exorcising of chronic malaise, heavy fog draped, over my bewildered, transfixed essence. O to breathe the sublime passages, inhaling the bequeathed lotus locus with you, friends akin, in the skin. United beneath a radical star radiating roof. O Yes! I am weaving a delicate spider web, of hope.

On the verge of merging with my portrait, the hue of my iris, Siamese blue. Suspended against these sky orbs, the crescent moon anvil striking pupils, of my tellurium tree hugging species. Like the generous creamery, of tawny, creamy, stipple, swarthy, clover sweet breath, twisting horned, goats. Horizontal UFO floating foreboding pupils, against jade sky. (Cats, the next to be hexed, written on the witching hour list.) Satan already portrait portrayed, horned as the horned moon, goatish goatee, cleft hooves. For to manifest as striking, is a nursing paps fecund hyena multiplying curse. Worse, to further fit the suspect list, my Venetian blind shut eyes, not pulley squeaking sliding open, like most pilgrim's eye slats, slanting ajar, at the boom of mornings' garish Cyclops eye. Mine flicker, doll's eye roll back, under the lashless slits, shut tight. Until the equipoised on one blue bamboo stalk, twin heron staring back from the starry firebug water, snow dusted herons sleep. The avis native sorceress, Pleiaides sparkle dripping pose, having heated the ice thawed. Glinting flake repellant, layered pinion vest, investing the ceremonial bird, impervious to the cold blooded cold.

And the revealing, peeling her clothes, and under garments off, like mummy wrappings. Nightingale fife piping Lilith, released from the golden ray cage of the sun. Naked blue apple hanging by a whisper, twilight.

The case rests, witness attests, arrest that cat! When sworn in, the pentagrams on his paws, fired tongues of smoke, rolled from the lawful bible. Hence, no defense, need be presented. This whiskered creature, is joined at the hip with the fire eater. Satan possessed, serpent hissing, heathen howling, (when a female is in heat, to be heart strings connected, to her fiery fertile forge...(Especially in the frost lion biting zero zero). Spitting scratching, having sold my soul, in liege, league with Beelzebub, my cat suit tinted pajama red. O please! Not to mention my gypsy guitar strumming, scarlet hood humming bird darting, stray pollinating ways. Mormon impregnated, pussy willow livery wivery stable of combined concubines. Contaminating damning me, as a hell raising heretic!

Adding to the minus minus tabbying tabulations, equaling a positive plus. For as a totemic tribe, we are a little tiger fur covered, padded feet vehicle, driving in backward, banned from Eden, stuck in our own hooked consummations.

Barring, disregarding, the jester jingling, octopus hat armed cards, of shame and blame. Let it be satellite orbited, that I furry chest roseate provide, for my stripey orange, stippled, swart, birch white, part Siamese, radiant families, with swaggering gratuity. When the world is naught, caught in the rusted lock jaw spiked, sprocket clockwork, docking tocking machinery, of the arresting Winter Witch.) At witch benumbing, intruding interlude, I switch. To bagging nippy, tail wagging rodents, treking snow shoed across, the Queen Ann's lace spinning, from the albino bee swarming, flecked sky. Of the hibernating, cloud shrouded, fortuitous (when waking ) white, chromite three hundred eyed, snoring frost dragon. But when the green witch springs into the dripping green spring; I am happy slapping fish from rain wrinkled ponds, brimming rivers, and the briny seaweed tumbling, hippocampus whinnying, horse powered tail swinging, cantos singing sea. Assiduously fish factory dropping, thick lipped, silver corselette, wriggling wigglers, with a stash of smaller fish, cache swallowed inside. Like diminishing in size, consumed in the pregnant belly of the bigger, Russian painted bird nesting dolls. (A Darwinian expost facto expose) Rich brocade laid, at the dainty lioness feet, of my courted from behind, purring riant paramours, and their pap clinging teeth in gums, pampered papooses. Grocery boy delivering, in spite of snow sleet rain heat, fresh goods martyred in my pitchfork teeth, to the Madame smorgasbord, Cat House of the poppy scarlet fevered moon. The prime, organs in tact, nurturing milk stirring, offerings, donated by your blue tuxedo, incognito. Albeit, the doting queen, vicious pernicious lioness mothers, fleet of mind teeth and feet, wile with plush "mink," trim slim limb style. Convoying any of many, grain plump vermin, skittering across the barn's barbaric gambit gamboling gamut. To the hay manger lullaby nursery, of her fur wrapped baby buntings. Blessed by Holy Bast.

I, Lazarus purr furring, the alluring, "Saint Joan of Arc" hydra slaying, claw bladed, feminine feminist, independent streaked minx. Myself, one of the dance with the devil in the pale moonlight, honored cognate fathers. As we cats, thank Bast, do not paint tainted scarlet letter A's to hang, wearily stone weighted, about our mates' sonorous necks. Fervid romancing, fertile females can bear, wear the scion litter of several fortune fortunate fathers. Each heir, seed spiraling into pyramid eared, sphinx, lynx feline fetus, wrapped within its own transparent umbilical attached sack. Indeed, such is the dynasty sophistication of our salubrious breeding breed.

And let it be tabbying fishwife proclaimed, minus a mirage corsage, that none of my mini me kits, (that's how we know whose are witch, the fleck of spots, the seven hang loose toes, the striped, swarthy, or birch white tots), transported by their loose flesh necks, clutched in the mothers' visceral gripped mouth.

Have never ever, in any wary life of mine, been forceps metal tongs dragged drugged, fish hook snared from the kitten shared socks kicking, full moon rhythmic, emptying womb lair. Daring a Cassandra doom "Beware" prophesy, to rear up its ugly head. Mourning the dented lopsided, scrawny unsupportable neck, palsied paralyzed, blank Jesus crucifix fish eyed, "delayed" baby. Who, in this iron forged teeth of the missile church. Mad Meg, scent tracking, frothing hyena pack, cold smoking state, of "kill you if I can;" too weak to huddling sib, Madonna teat suckle. Would not live until nacreous dusk; parting the same rueful, blushing with shame day, that vulturously exodus ushered him, mangled lamb forth.

As a caring father, thank Bast, I do not carry this blood draining fate, of added guilt and grievous, Atlas holding up the world, weight.

I, Lazarus, bleeding roses, annealed by age, into shielding thorns. Supplication sustained, by the confluent voices, of the legs, sheathed beneath glittering double fish tail, spindrift salient mermaids. Siren soprano, luminous phosphorous rising, over the merciless, nacre reliquary, green sheen matutinal, nocturnal, cat's cradle rocking sea. Apace in each rip tooth age, sheltered by crannies and nooks. And the maverick candor of those graced with kindness; the boon of a magenta bloom, survives in every anemic age.

I who broom banish gloom, by the apotheosis presence of my totemic, totaling family. That I can be suddenly conscripted, eradicated from. When called by the mute tongueless, club footed, goblin daughter. Tree stump tripping messenger, of unbalanced destiny.

Untimely rising again, by the pyramid sphinx of my anchoring religion, the grand dam, damask rose, Bast, for as long as forever is.

Pensively enduring in this blurring, antlered red hart fleeing, poison arrow tip strung, austere fear ridden, scapegoat driven, present – past. Above ancient cloud meditating rocks, cave coves, of the turquoise coasting coast. Dreaming thinking, weeping creeping. Camouflaging, blending into lunar owl winged, hunting shadows (as readily as a white gloved, rippling with extra finger extensions, blue tuxedo cat can. Hand and glove, paw and hand, fitting into fellowship, with the invisible man.

## MONKEY BLOOD

Monkey Blood O Monkey Blood
indeed he was
a piece of work!
With his shoe shining monkeyshines, frantic chattering antics,
his eyes were the eye of the Hurry Cane, lightening bolts for pupils
fiendishly ignited
as a pupil
of everything
that flashes and shines.
Discarded disregarded  tinfoil
gum  wrappers
tossed glittering silvery in the street,
awe-
struck him Ouch!
His constant deluge of epiphanies, sniffing nosiness
at the insignifigant,
Made him seem like he was just born, (or a mindless idiot.)
An impetuous teen spirit,
Though the fury of his electric blue blood
had boiled in the recoiling sun
for more than half a century.
Wound up too tight
with a brand new silver shiny key,
ready to spring into action
as a cymbol clashing toy decoy
for those who were trying to.
This crocodile grinning
Voodoo child,
who wept crocodile tears.
A whizz at interpreting symbols, being a broken hybrid bred symbol, breed of himself
inbreed of a cotton pickin, Cotton Ball southern lineage, Y'all.
Interrupting dullish doltish conversations
he was dude not included in, rattling metaphoric symbols off like rattling pots and pans
in some floating astro sailor's kitchen,
until someone blew a fuse
or a poison dart, at his darting nimble apish shape.

It's no use, there's no excuse, Confucious says, he lives to confuse.
But his Opelia floating down the river loopy rhyming communions, performed with method to the madne
at odds with circumstance
because,
they shivery timbers scare him
with their stern thin Gila Monster lips, skin tight or sagging frowning eye slits
make him pant dance and itch, rip him from his bones
you see
distancing
is
his atomic weapon,
setting himself up for rejection.
A unicycle bi pedal pedaling misanthrope
for small change
there is no hope.
Monkey Blood O Monkey Blood
tattooed with spine tapping seizing stories
up and down his  shaved fur limbs
and sunken little manly chest,
detailing even his tail
he bit off during a panic attack.
A Lucy in the Skies, Big Dipper naked ape
psychedlic voodoo child, cunning funning freak.


2
Ladies and gentlemen
the elephant trumpeting circus crushed velvet curtain opens to reveal
This live wire cannon blasted stunt
shot from an ambulance wailing past!
Monkey blood, injected with knock out narcotics, tied into a padded straightjacket
ordered by his unwrapped Mummy, to keep him pajama warm,
for alas he was
pistil muzzle stuck, in a goosebumps past so cold, it freezied off a witch's tits.
An unsung hero, heroine chained in Tom Bedlam's dungeon, with window bars
And two winking bi polar stars, floating over his renegade head.
O what to do O what to do
with Voodoo child, Little Monkey Blood
who wore an inverted razor suit and bled acid blood.
Poor Monkey Blood Poor Monkey Blood

Like a sock monkey in a shock shop, gift wrapped
at state hospital, the cement floor stretched so glacial thick,
not even a crack for a weed to grow through.
Slammed behind a locked metal door, with murderers, the criminally insane and who knows who
bunking with funky Monkey Blood, who could only gnash his teeth, as harmless as a fowl, hanging
like a limp biscuit
From the foxe's mouth.
Of course this made him a mental gimp, a mentally limping gimp
with only his Monkey Blood antics for defense.
O what fowl was fair made hairless here?
His face fast being erased
from WHAT outside interference.
But Monkey Blood, reputed for his Houdini escapes
since he was a bouncy baby, disappearing from his lock in pen
without a track of trace
learned to time travel, resurfacing on a Calif. Pink sand beach, tatooed with real surreal flaming
giraffe galloping tales
that got to sun themselves in the arms of the sun wearing shades, and swim in the peaceful
turquoise sea
the lapping laughing turquoise sea.
By the whale song seal clapping ocean, he met a man with twilight eyes, blue beard goatee
who could see below the surface of the kinetic surfing Monkey Blood.
An artist by trade, who could paint the world any shade,
that blue eyed visionary
knew who She wuz, for heaven's sake he was a She!
Taught her to believe, that fuzz less wuss
O Monkey Blood O Monkey Blood
because of the ties with a circus past, drinks water until drunk from a cup
reflecting dazzling lights, revolving ferris wheel,
likes to offer the magic cup to you. Wishes to share, his flapping tail fish out of water
tales too, stone released flapping gargoyles, flashing shining tinfoil dream scenes.
At home
He She pirouhettes through ankle beaded grass, of Henri Rousseau's Carnival Night,
beneath a spoonful of full moon, dressed in the white silk clown suit, wearing slippers
made of silver moon slivers too,
and the silk white dunce hat, pointing at the white silk hidden star, star swept night.

# VIOLET

The seven
ray arrayed
demoiselles:
Orange Yellow
Green Red
Indigo Blue
Violet.
Their prismatic sister ship,
like a parade of Easter eggs
made of tomorrow's marrow,
tied
color dyed
by rainbow tides
splashing flashing from the Tiger
striped tropical sun.
Their flesh, hair, eyes,
the radical radiance of
blazing shadeless shades.
Submarine submerged
in their own
Apollo appointed
risque racy
sheen.

The boundless boundaries
of the wreck less rushing sea,
swaying spraying
scaly crocodile wrestling waves,
specular reflecting, each painted sister's
color glazed horse;
its skeleton forming,
breaking free, from Poisedon's coral shoulder,
growing flesh over bone,
their untainted color coats.
How now, born into solid 3d form,
rearing Phoenix rising from the prism

roaring tides,
tangible pulsing pagan horses
swimming, swan gliding
to the edge of
the ship wreck shore.

These dazzling Colleens,
reined and routed by Violet
astride her violet force horse,
reminiscent of the nascent
raging wild girl
with her unchained tiger spirit
in Rousseau's painting, "War."

Her star spiked violet hair,
sticking out in needle points
from her radiant dome.
Gymnastically acrobatically
circus balanced, (like the painting girl)
standing on the violet blooming back
of her hale and halcyon booming
haled horse,
its violet mane and trumpeting tail.
The horse sticking out
its unbridled
violet sweating tongue.

Blasting through a conch shell, (the kind used
to plug in, and radiate from its glossy, pleasing
pink shell, a child's appeasing nite light.)
General Violet,
commandeering her regal ranks
to mount each matched horse.
Then a violet scented wind
mercurial ushers
through their sea horse ears,
the primal flight
of lusterous pearl hooves.
Clip clop clip clop

trit trot trit trot
trotting,
imprinting swirling prints
across the impressionable, rainbow
streaked beach.

Look!
Up above the skeleton enmeshed reef
the color comrades point.
Oh! Oh! Oh! See!
The mermaid fetus gilled moon
swim upstream the sky!
Oh how this moon child grows!
as it Eastern Easterly rises
into a bone chilling angel
baring its glaring wolf teeth.
Then with white tuxedo
elegance, effulgence,
it becomes the wan
moon tailed man,
seven out stretched arms
and wrists
connected to
his color magnet hands
attracting
negative subtracting
colors
to absence.
His negating gamut
protege aided by
the white gowned
Angel fierce,
with a stalactite bite
succubus sucking in
erasing matrix shades;
a demonic duo
ally aligned
until the turquoise twilight sky
is delivered

demoiselle crane white.

Their world devoid of tints and hues,
dragging tails and hooves,
seven lugubrious
rice white ponies
Yawn,
drawn back into the crooning sea,
melt into its cradling womb.
See you manana
sleepy horses,
when you rise
corralled by coral,
the stars still alive
after the dome slides shut
over the chromatic
daytime sky.

As
Lo! Looky here!
The seven flashing
sisters
are strippers,
tapped zapped,
shedding their
sumptuous hues.

Though
All living colors were killed
smote,
no blood
bled,
no tears
of fear
were shed.
Now the seven  heavenly sisters,
their faces
like powdered white Geisha girls,
ceremoniously bow

kow-tow
before the ageless
Andromeda polished
castle
of the grave less deathless
tilted hourglass
night
of the white salamanders,
dragon frozen
on the gargoyle eves
of the moon marble palatial palace;

of this lotus white whirling
woe-be-gone primitive eve;
where even ancient bone dust spirits
clone each others
heart laugh,
earless ears
hearing the tinkle tinkle tinkle
of bells,
mirth echos
ringing across light years.

Flakes of moon dust
stirred up
from the Fred Astaire
hot foot
dancing prancing
moon tailed man;
assailing the sisters'
exposed below,
their white fringe lashes
lashing batting
fanning flakes,
away from
their open wide
dove white iris.

Hello

seven day sisters
of this glowing ermine esprit night,
shielded by the pianissimo
aura of white light,
Polar bear immune
to the scaly crested ivory dragon
back bone
of the cold,
bleeding frosty smoke in air.
Wind notes chiming through its ribs,
crested head first, it treks
slippery glass stairs downward
on mountain spiked boot claws,
leaving its spiraling mountain lair
on the jagged edge of air.
Hypnotized mesmerized
the coldblooded cold
stares
at the sisters' glowing starfish
hands.
Dares to share
in their demoiselle ceremonial
white crane
dance,
his spiked whip tail
dog curled around his true blue feet,
grinning a harvest of icicle scythe teeth,
all eyes

As the lunar geisha girls
unplait
their white seal sleek
hair released,
comet tail sweeping
to their unbound
rabbit bone delicate
naked feet.

Here,

Invisible to eyes,
behind the towering
enlightened temperament
of this moon marble temple retreat;
with the white rain
sleeting snow;
giggling and shadowless,
lacking that
constant diurnal
thin shade friend,
but each, as the other
instead,
seated, lotus style
in the snow,
yet they do not get wet.
By a seventh sense,
two agile fingers
directing
dynasty carved
bone sticks,
they eat with by dipping,
lifting the snow
heaped
on China white plates;
offering the back bone of the tingling cold
ivory dragon
breathing frost and mist,
its own snow dish.

Then the white lotus
snow eaters,
yogi slowly
breathe,
transitioning transmorphing
into demoiselle snow feathered cranes
sprinting on extended
chopstick thin legs,
elevating
lifting the legs to tuck beneath tufts,

as they sail beyond beyond;
clock hands
tornado spinning
counterclockwise
past the past of
tomorrow's future,
stars dotting
the clock's glass face.
Whizzing past light years,
seven heavenly daughters
of Atlas,
reach the Pleiades constellation,
their rice white geisha faces
flashing illumination
through icy
cold cube
stars.

At the Sirius signal,
the Dog Star
leaps in bounds,
to the other side
of the Pierrot white pony
spinning carousel night.
At the dawn of the sun
in its morning glory,
the sisters' color comrade ride
astride the living color
sun beam tigers,
cubs of the Mother Tiger striped sun,
(her fawned offspring
with stained glass keen claws)
jungle lunging
to this new birth of planet earth.

At the shore of the tumbling prism breakers,
reborn in the blaze
every colt, placenta delivered
morning;

seven spectrum horses
rear up on pearly hooves
shaking out their salt water licked manes,
nuzzling forward to lick the hands
of Violet's religious legion of light.

So Fly on! Damoseille snowy crane sisters
of the dragon tingling night!
Ride! Chromatic comrades on the charging backs
of the flashing rip tide sun cubs,
in your cyclical revolving flight.
Seven sisters
of the coral bone,
pure color coated,
prism eyed horses!
Atlas daughters
of the Pleiades,
your indomitable faces,
blazing through
icy
cube stars
in space.

# TREVOR'S SONG

The cat's got my tongue
so I cannot talk,
though the words
leaping flipper dugong
shine behind
my glowing
U F O skull
taunting haunting me,
then notched tail gone,
Bermuda Triangle
disappear,
when the radar over heats
in my north of south
tropical hurricane brain
that cannot seem to uncover
the missing Jack Skeleton
key
buried like pirate treasure.

To my own grinning chagrin,
even
ear less
pastiche Mohawk plumed
pirate skulking
madcap
hopping
orange circle cheek
bone cracking
nuts
beak,
Venus fly trap
jungle blooming
spectrum booming
stupid Narcissistic cupid
mirror heart peering
preening

parrots can talk,
in squawking
human voices.

Though I am dumb,
I'm not so dumb
as you may think.
My head is a camera
flashing snapshots,
krypton kryptonite
atomic number
waiting
to regenerate,
using total recall
to link
the transmitted pictures
in sequential order
from any time
past present

and the future

I can red eye of the seething cauldron read
by brain surging
surfing cosmic
Yin Yang
Chee
wheeling
magnetic energy.

The transmutable green gray eyed
candle hatted, orange goatee
Vincent
in his mute
but intensely communicative
vortex flux layered paintings
that hold viewers
speechless,

could see
along with me

the same
gyromagnetic
falcon swooping wing
potent forces
that seize

the gloaming foaming red tides;
like the shell hoofed red bulls
lowering coral horns
to chase
the boneless unicorn waves
heaving to leap
higher higher,
tower twirling staircase horns
liquid spirited
phantom swords,
attacking the sky
in rebellion,
until they crash and break.

Is it then
this unicorn hunting
Salem assailant
malign magnetism
that freezes me from others?
Allied tied with the hair raising
writhing
snake hair hissing
Gorgon sisters,
whose Medusa Martian
red eyes, target me
turning my tongue
to stone;
by eclipsing
the positive
sphinx staring suns

Cyclops blinded,
to Hell spell
foster their own
limbless
nefarious
spiked
needle headed child
to conquer,
spread their Satanic necrophilia
tumor diseased
humor.

But in spite of being
outcast cast,
there are those
who love
believe in me,
so I try to tune
my tunnel echoing ears
to hear their spoken air messages,
though I can be blind as a snowstorm,
deaf as a broken bell,
when I am somewhere else
beyond this jar capped world.

Because my disobedient
body jerks,
I flap my hands
chew on shirts,
jabber voice box quioxtic sounds
so I sound like the poor fool
Tom Bedlam,
parrot mirror words,
bang things against
my protruding teeth,
I guess I look
clown like too,
like the madcap jingling
flapping parrots.

But make no mistake,
teach me not
what I taught myself
when I toddler walked,
but how
you
can reach
the telepathic
encyclopedic volumes
that I have
sphinx sun eyes
solar pyramid
cache stashed.

# Poem 2

For Trevor's parents; Tom and Michelle Castro

A little wild
a little tame;
Mother,
don't worry
someday I'll claim
the quicksilver ring
that keeps safe my mercurial words.
The ballet leaping frog prince
wears it as a crown
on his spotted bald green head.
His slit mouth unhinged
twilight twinkles his keen little teeth,
from his balloon sack
he proudly emits
deep kingly croaks Re deep! Re deep!

During the day
he keeps the ring
buoyed
in a rainbow bubble
that does not pop.

Slips his slippery
seaweed slimy
pea green
dotted hands,
through the slippery firm, transparent wall
that heals, seals itself shut again,
to take
then return
when dawn gongs the ring reigning treasure.
He blew this burst proof bubble
from the bog elemental
green reed pipe,
stashed beneath
his pond ring lily pad throne.

After I steal the ring back
off his leopard spotted lime crown,
(he wears it at the dawn of
luminous peach sundown,
and all through the blinky firefly festival
he unwittingly believes  he commandeers
wearing the dazzling crown.

When I hold
the Golem precious
collapsed star
shivering sliver
mercury encasing
my flowing knowing words;
then will I tell you
how
I've loved you since
I grew my mirror echoing ears,
my jungle jade cat eyes
like yours,
a little wild
a little tame

My mother
Michelle Lorri,
whose clever hands are two feathered swans
when she strokes my face,
for me is the naked white morning
stretched across dewy blue fields,
her cascading river hair
splashing over the hills of her shoulders.
Whose pyramid eyes
see visions
like mine,
that she Luna moth
captures on canvass;
who's there for me
when she is not,
in her Pegasus fluttering absence.

Tom is my father
wears a thinker's hat
navigating the abstract,
unchartered dimensions,
but becomes a Mediterranean
swashbuckling pirate
when defending tongueless me.
Both mom and he
locomotive smoking bulls,
hooves splaying dirt
lower thick wishbone curved horns,
when I am mountain lion threatened.
Myself the mooing moon calf
nuzzling between their gentle fur,
their clover sweet muzzles.

Dad's helix spiraling, black comet hair
matches mine,
his tinkering tooling long fingers,
the ark and sway of his body.

He who architect flashlight focuses
numeralogically
calculating the possible
patterns
of unknown constellations.

When the Titan shadow night
has stepped out of its hosts'
colossal
mass,
rustling through the spiny ferns and shoots,
swinging my sing song swing,
tapping barking fingers
at my glass window door

Then I charge between my glowing parents
under the body warm sheets.
Tick tock
inside the silence,
within her mermaid head,
I can read
Mom's houses of pictures,
iridescent phosphorescent
pearly blind ponies of see.

Tick tock tick tock
Dads' black mice whiskered numbers
piling on cheerleader piggy back style
pyramiding
to the forbidding stars.
Comforter wrapped
in the breathing essence
of their presence.

Somewhere behind
a curtain of air
I fly out of my clumsy body
and I am the man in the wind,

my airy fingers ruffling, petting
the black swans' feathers,
their crimson sun eyes closed
in a floating repose.
Me gently rocking them
like delicate sylph necked
black snow boats,
as I gypsy breeze tickle
concentric circles
across the sleeping black lake.

# III

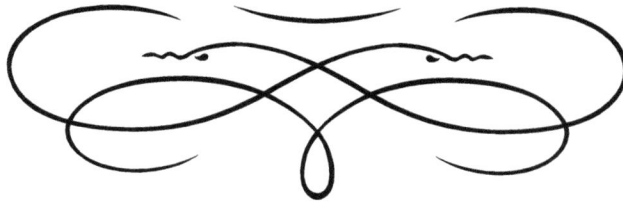

# THE TWINS

Under the gazing gems
of the Gemini geminus
dazzling blue star twins,
the bowing star dusted boughs
of candle needle pine scented pines,
seasonally conjoined
conical green canonbaums
dwarf fur hatted topmost tips
of the totem tolling tokens,
trimming rimming
the boundless boundaries
of these echo haunted
terrestrial inhabited
wolf child wilds,
pointed nose
open throat vibrating
melancholy choir melody
fluidly
reaching the supreme Enubis ears
of the pure, golden furred
She wolf
Diva
born on the solo satellite, (like Venus oceanic rising, in her pearl jam fluted scallop shell)
blood tears flooding her eyes
as she recognizes
the golden tongue
flattened ear
sweeping bough tailed
diamond skull
quadrupeds
of her topaz fluid worshiping tribe.
Through her theater fringed golden lashes
moon eyes staring
downward
earthward
at her perennial soprano tenor wailing wards

sorcery crafting a pervasive bewailing grief
sending bone chilling shivers down the spines
of even the blind egg encapsulated
golden eagles
that have not yet beaked or clawed
through their calcified dome homes,
commencing cognizance, of the azure blue horse sky
galloping beyond the heartwood trees,
to luster glance in ice statue trance
at the Saturn glowing ringed
Fire bird comet tailed
entrance to infinity,
above the revolving evolving
omnipresent potent
Mona Lisa staring moon,
where untamed phenomenons
often sphinx riddle occur below.


2
Just as
One bereaving
hungry grieving
moaning wind
pine wreathed
pining evening; (nexus bonded with Romulus and Remus,
of Nero's mad eye of the hurry cane! fiddling fury, falling fire torched Rome)
feasibly forsaken (though not in view of any eyes but the lonely She wolf's on the moon)
by a faceless form,
dracontic cyclical Gibbous
moon veiled by the She wolf's dark side,
though not possessed by the procession of
a trailing husband claimed, wedding veil train.
A forlorn bewailing mother child
and this dark daughter's preveiling erred heir;
torn by family and steeple pointing, harlot
church
over the ill begotten curse
she unalterably left

on her own

sugar footed pony.
The debased unchaste
storm plagued
lightening chased,
sparking zigzag fragments of the matrix golden bone bolts,
almost teasingly
magnetic field clinging to
but not piercing
this lost Wendy bird,
this melon headed
flailing pumping her twiggy arms,
gamin mud lark
cuckoo bird,
starving Raven fallen
from the haven nest

or dropped
from a carriage wheeling
asteroid, before it exploded, meteor crashed,
onto the back of the turquoise midnight blue
Gemini star branded pony,
with splashing cresting
curling wavelets
manely
King of the Wind and Air
waterfall splashing lashing across
its golden river gliding neck.
The ghostly white
coyote
howling baby
cowgirl;
get along lil' doggie,
lil' blue vein rivering
rubber boned
contortionist,
candle skulled
crisscrossed

always lost
disoriented spinning compass
polarized between:
The Tropic of Cancer
and the Tropic of Thermal Underwear
mountain bearded
horned Capricorn bearded
octopus suction cup
gum shoe hooves,
Spider Man gripping.
The Satanic but guileless goats,
never tipping tripping off
the lung huffing, oxygen thin
miles high craggy face glazed zenith,
jutting through the pregnant snow fury
stored in the furry black sheep clouds,
slippery sloped
hoof speared sphere.

These dueling hemispheres (of right or wrong, right of left, up or down)
the dyslectic directionless sister kid
palomino between; (later action actualized, when she was able to point
her tiny pink pointer finger towards Mr. Nobody's quagmire quicksand marsh,
each time she tried to Mistress Silver Plum Empress rule, dominate her misleading reign,
though the sugar footed pony was rein less.)

To the minus zero degree, moth to a light bulb singed wing dazed, confused
dumb numbed,
with no suspicions
of auspicious aviary winged talents hidden,
deficient of any wakeful trace
of Amelia Earhart's
proficient
intrinsically inherit
skyward or terrestrial map zone sense
written in stone by chromosomes.
Totally Not
gingerbread inbred
in this disinherited

backwards sailing
wingless navigator (in the bundled beginning, nursed by any empathetic wet nurse
milk teated mamma
mammal, along the Milky Way, including altruistic contagious mother rats, plagued
by their own gannet screeching, voracious rat nest breeding, breathing incubators, still
donating their creamy creameries, and morally questionable, night stalking the beneficent
rats, sleek street walkers, the harpie screeching cats, giving suck in ample bra-less four
nipple double breasted silk milk supply, to the oddly mewing hairless newbie. These wet
nurse nursery nursers, all milk bank Heaven bound Saints, whether or not the church
pointed its steeple, harlot accusingly, at their wayward pussy cat ways!

These milk bar nourishers, rewarded by a bite or lick off the sugar hearted pony's sugar
hooves. And like the shark, that can replace an entire set of teeth, the pony's hooves
regenerated any missing cubes in the sugar sweet sweet feet. Also on the plush plus side,
all this mother bear generosity honey spread,
at least shut the siren screeching fur less, wretched wrinkly red faced, pink lung powered
hungry thing up! So diurnal tribes were blessed with deep Sand man sleep, and the others
continued with their meteor eyed feats.)

Though unbeknownst to stocking shadow kingdoms,
the ruby fire eyed ruling
sovereign zodiacal Tiger flashing lightening from its claws
while leaping from Tiger blazing island stars,
Magi gifted the "steady now" pony's snowy cube shoes
with prancing prowess,
the genie genius
of Capricorn mountain Goat feral God
octopus suction cup plunging shoes,
legally regally unyieldingly sure footed
so the Gemini blue pony
did not slip slide,
or bush thrashing crash
crushing the daisy petal
cargo.

As time skipped rope, eloped with the secret neonate,
leaving the silky haired spirited brook babbling
Queen Mab, whose commandeering commands
fell on deaf ears,

as the day gold pony
forgot not the leaf disguised wind
of any wind shoed path,
and Tiger sniffed
the way
through fog distorted, Hecate forked
and disjointed tracks.

3
Though the saddle her rocking cradle,
holding on to the horn
with no regrets, about the whirring blue dragon fly fly away day,
as the Gemini star leashed pony
sailed and flashed through the wind woods,
fiendishly stalked by a friendly
Shadow
did not follow the tot.

When the pony stretched her Ubangi neck
to drink in the leopard green
Narcissus miming rhyming
River
drank the pony in
with the ferny red banks;

but the grass haired baby
on the spirit pony's back
bankrupted,
her reflection
drew a  blank,
proposing the questing question of
was she for real or not?

4
For this summer gypsy moth baby
zephyr breathing
baby's breath indigo iris child,
summer ripe blueberry girl,
it was green blue and gold, summer forever

straddling her rabbit eared bunny soft pony,
wearing her rain hat sun hat
cloud hat
hat less
under the Atlas mapped
ardent spirited
atmospheric ambiance,
mosquito hawk preying mantis
escorted in on web thread whisker wispy legs;

her standing up straight grass hair
swaying under the priestly owl's
black rainbow
swift
wing wind levitating sails.

The big dipper
dipping into the deep night cauldron
ladling out
slews of star stews,
From the ship of her pony
she cast out a line
reeling in Rainbow fish, Angel puckering fish
from the wooden shoe rocking
starry abyss,
setting her catch to fry
in tomorrow's
unyoked yellow ox fire horned sun.

Her bone bridge
growing bigger bolder
as the shadowed sun grew distant, colder,
and though she called for her eyeless earless
Shadow could not hear,
could not see to seek her.
And in the turtle paddling river
her own cardinal pastel presence
did not mermaid swim to her
or reach for her reassuringly
when she reached.

Still the golden fur
of the She wolf
spread out beneath her
pink rabbit delicate feet,
and the wolf mother
kept a monolithic wake
over the raven waif

with a star between her green leaping Tiger eyes,
(paw planted there, as a glittery mark from the star deluged cosmic Tiger)
in her birthday glowing tangelo yellow
sunrise
tangerine submarine
satiny supple suit.
This bare- ly big enough
to boot
that prickly root
lil' rhubarb,
wearing
no cowgirl boots—

5
Yet as the puzzling myth of the fur less
found foundling,
swan trumpeted,tweeted spread
like a fanned forest fire
to the silky ear flocks
of silo towering towns,
the black sheep bannered together
shaved
saved and gave
a sack of
curly back fleece (for their mischanced black sheep symbolic niece)
to the motherly red kerchief hens
who knitted  wooly black sheep
booties (to keep her ten wiggly piggies warm
with enough left over for small hand socks and a fountain head cover)
sewing machine heads bobbing
with a peck and jerk

from scissor beaks
and spinning wheel wool winding feet.

This gamin expanding her gamut
of jasmine hearted beasts
waiving the laws
of jungle crocodile feast,
touched by her nativity needs
a babe without a barn
naivety.

Even in the pine sky pointing ranges
a reflective bear cub
sensing the snow Queen's ascending scent,
wrinkled his loose skin forehead em pathetically,
unzipped his own berry furry suit,
presented it to her
of a lesser God
than the Great Sky Bear he thought,
witch she, the shivery timbers tot
slipped into
snug as a snail,
or a sleepy cucumber
during a blustery creeping shadow spell.
Though the generous cub
sprouted blazed raised radiated
the spreading forest fur points of another
when the brindle miffed mother glared,
quicker thicker than the latter
to golden ladder up
the ice flecked skies,
meet with the illustrious Canis Major.

O The blue pony's unreined
shadowless shadow child,
made of backbone and porcupine spine.
A little robber girl,
stealing future less eggs
sucked out the embryonic yolks

with hungry animal lips
ate beetles spiders and fish.
After all she did not create
the weaker species gets eaten,
the unjust justice
of canabolism,
but she did learn to funeral mourn it.

The she without a name
cat eyes
eagle eyes
evil eye
falcon shadow hunting
on roller skating
sky wings,
sweeping across blue vapors
ponied on her survival conception,
hunting for the blind
deaf and dumb
Shadow,
and her carnal body blood cheeked
turtle river
mermaid twin

On this golden geese
with snake slender necks
bearing golden jingling key rings,
feather finger opening
to new climatic climates,
doors to perceptive dimensions,
a migrating gypsy
pony driven wagon less carnival
journey
beneath the blazing yellow bull horned sun
pulling its deity sized thundering wagon
of illuminated flashing swords
that plunge into its trudging body
shooting the cardinal red blood leaking
from the bull stabbed sun,

toiling east to west across the never stumbling
sacrificial tolling reincarnate skies,
and the dueling domino torches
of the dragon eyed Gemini twins;
a transcendental metamorphosis
O Time
slowly transforming her
from a grubbing baby
draped in leaves and dirt,
her green apple night rise transparent painted skin,
the growing glowing inchworm
mummy bandaged,
chrysalis unwrapped,
larva to jewel eyed fly
out she popped
flew out of stagnant water,
a Tiger green eyed woman,
bathed in lavender mulberry
blossoms,
part free love
milk bank sainted rat,
mercenary feral prowling yowling cat,
part Rainbow Angel kissing fish.
Animal instinctual
part golden palomino pony
whose unconditional love
was sweet as sugar plantations,
part echoing wailing amber feathered coyote,
a leaping black sheep.
The golden She wolf
stranded on the revolving moon
having born witness
to the evolution
of the child's revolution
sphinx riddling fate;
encompassed concealed
within an unbreakable shell
the golden eagle's germinating chick,
as far as two eyed human people

were deaf dumb and blind
dead to her.

Who was she?
no shadow gypsy moth
sailing behind beside or under her nomadic mapped feet,
(like some cryptic protracting clawed vampire
sleeping in an unnailed creaking pine coffin
until the glass stabbing
rays of daylight deceased)
as no reflecting surface
mirror married
her painted image
to her solo
blood cheeked source.

# GOAT BOY

The hunt for the unicorn white night nuptial
beneath the ivory tortoise shell moon
as she climbs
laying phosphorous eggs
buried in the evanesce dust of dusk
rocket elevating
dispelling
exposing the galactic eggs against
the wandering nomad phthalocyanine Giant (like salt glittering starfish, naked against the foamy
beach, tides retreating to the pulsing whirlpool cyclops eye of the colossal Titan sea )
and the Gemini star struck twins
alien united, beyond the scorpion sting of terrestrial woes,
navigator charted, sanguine between; Cancer's tame monstrous crab star teeth claws,
and the gem horned bull, Taurus,
cousin to the fire horned red bull sun,
cousin to the blue
ring nose bull, of the zebra striped, solar sessional, somnolent transitional pastures.
Patchwork patched by Martian fields
of crucified dried and dying Sun flowers
no longer able to lift their yellow crowned faces
on spiny neck stem stalks, their flapping in the green sleeves rustling breeze, uniquely palm diagram
oracle leaf hands,
following the potent intransigent red bull wagon hauling sun's
travailing journey across its east to west, set in Stonehenge stone
sea towering sylvan meadow path
its fire horns blazing.

But it will always be a meadow
where the meadow lark pipes her Nightingale fire song through the burning rushes,
where he shifted feet hopping, playing his flute of bone, continuing the sequential melodic
consciousness
of the lively goat who once leaped on the resonating hollow leg bone, he piper piped the skylark
yellow breasted rising rain of notes from.
Whether it was a maroon or blue meadow, a gold meadow, a dried meadow spawning the brutal
spiked crucified Sunflower parched harsh crowns,
an emerald foxfire flashing phosphorescent meadow,

or an erogenous winter fox white furred meadow,
is inconsequential, transcendental and left entirely to his moody reasoning,
as his name was Meadow,
where she met him I mean,
the goateed Goat boy that is
was the infusing primal fountain head of the seasons in rapid flux,
witch ever suited him best, he chose.
He was dressed, if he was dressed,
the green leaf suit, might have been a mirage (like the fleeting, lime green gecko darting, heart leaf
floating lily pads, blue eye glinting water paradise, hallucinated in sand man funneling sand into
his open mouthed indigo starry dream bag-twisted knotted closed tight with a silken rope, thirsting
dune, inflammable camel, water fueled in hilly humps territory.)
The goateed goats, like a shell horned, horn of plenty, miscellany opus, paramount atoll, of all racing
colors mixed, brindled speckled spotted, red blue verdant green, plum purple, standing out against
the paler side of the pale horizon less.
The goats four legged hooves, following the piper king in a sort of dancing tango, his musically
induced steps. The little bells around their necks tinkling dinging, like the happy bells were ringing
inside of the reindeer naked tree horned, or Gothic cathedral horned creatures, across the skylark
dreaming, Angora furred silky spinning secret snowing fur filling every furrow, crevice. Mate
arousing sensual naked lounging meadow, pregnant with unlatched unmatched nesting altars,
hidden evolutionary cradling nooks, unhooked crannies.
The Goat Boy eating not apples, instigators of serpent sapient sins in Edens, although this meadow
was a paragon of a heathen Eden, (in the Bacchus horny temptation of its bulging grape lust,
thrilling cut to the chase, minus the chase of the cinnamon fox killing hunt, non chaste virginal hilly
hills, accommodating dating mating rituals. Its Pan tantalizing tail wagging, begging to be tasted,
seed spun juicy fruit, offered from the heavy laden knuckle knob bed branches of gnarly dwarf trees)
but ripe black olives, witch he also hand fed to the eager bell ringing marshmallow mellow goats.

She hid behind the swaying sculpture of peacock tailed bushes
magnetized by his acute mastery of the many tongued flute,
his eyes reflecting an unknown (to her naivety) structure of monolithic upright and horizontal
dawning stones
against the unexplored blue timeless monolith timed Odyssey of twilight.

The current rhapsody in Cobalt Blue
of the spinning planet
draping the fairy fading evancse dust of twilight,
calling the bell tinkling singing
song of the marble eyed

twin horned
silky goats, their goatees flowing water
as they kneeled on padded knees
by a marsh pond
where a blue feathered heron
stood, eyelids folded over eyes
like a one legged praying blue angel.

Nearby the green goats dove peaceful sleep,
the Goat boy had engineered
a stone hugging stone tower (like Pompeii's bubbling volcano, vomited its pent up lava fury, like
people, stone hugging stone sister brother, seconds before the impending boiling wrath, swallowed
them forever)
with rock stepping staircase reaching the stars
witch he mounted up up to the towering zenith (as he was the strapping surefooted goat boy, with the
stubborn intrepid will of a goat)
witch eclipsed the rising sun and moon in their early ascensions.
On the plateau of the straight backed tower
he piped into the flute of bone
beckoning a whirl wind,
a flapping cloud of swarming bats.
If the creatures were blind,they could ingeniously see
by targeting sound waves,
creating order out of chaos,
the shepherded herd
eager to please,
taking positions in a formation
grasping clasping the straps on his back,
a Golgotha fluttering sea of wings
synergistic ally working as twin
Gargoyle Gargantua wings,
lifting him as he leapt
with burning thighs and brain
into his dream vision, the bonafide tides of Ariel apotheosized appendages, on looping swooping
leathery, rivering finger flight
O flying
as he circled the Angora furred snowing fur meadow
for he was the meadow,
the goateed Goat boy, artful illuminator, shepherding herder of the living,

piping the fluted consciousness
of the intersecting dead, roses booming through the eye holes of their discarded skulls,
their silky fur continuing to grow through the meadow
winds whistling through their broken bones,
the piping vessel he used, to release their transferred songs,
a testimony to his acutely Pan eared translations.

Yet he was now, wasn't he, the bat boy
as he did not waver cant or slant, in the bat congregational sensational DaVinci heights;
as he glided like a skater on ice
a smaller shadow shot across the welcoming welkin with him,
it was not pinned to the spinning ground
where Shadow Land thrived, shades surviving on the rustling ground zero.
She sensed who it belonged to at once,
for how do you not know your own feet in front of you,
their wet tracks behind you,
your own thin shadow child
who fetus slides out of your carnal body?

When the bat boy and her shadow sailed
like vessel virgins through water,
the clocks stopped,
but an hour glass would have emptied its funneling sandman glowing blue sand
hours ago,
by the time he prodigal returned to the roof of his gargoyle winged departure
suspended upside down like a mammoth bat
as the squeaking bats let loose, dispersing in a black snowing fury;
as the non doubting goat boy, trotted down the steep sides of the stone laid wall
meeting her shadow below, already holding hands with his own, waiting on ground zero for their guide
they veil sailed and slipped through rippling grass, he skipper skipping on golden bones
to the blue heron angel feathered pond
where the kneeling goats
dreamed of bearded bleating kids.

The sub solar green bearded Marchian pond
of subterranean arched passageways, leading to mossy hidey holes
covertly hidden in the silent under water
red slider turtles, emerald green limbless tadpoles, one special flickering morning
nubby arms and legs erupting, glittering fish breathing water,

neighboring neighbors of the swaying green algae lady
slippery fingers wrapped around rocks, bottom fish anchoring her,
keeper kept his smooth palette mixed with fluid permeating colors,
his tendril brush
cradled in her furry arms where she lay hovering,
fuzzy green felicitous rose
in the heron blessed pool
to the vision of his goateed face above,
re gifting him with what she keeper
kept hidden in wait for him.

Then with swift sure strokes he was painting
shadow's blossoming reflection in water,
but it was not the thin flat shadow he painted,
it was She, herself, in the trembling blue lioness awakening waters.

How did she know it was the renaissance of her own, wood sly elfina self
she had never eyed, as it simply was not there
to be captured in any mirroring marriage?
O the unicorn moon
pointed its true cosmic yen yang nuptial horn
at the flesh and salient blood cheeked woman
to heralded peaceful dove, tinkling goat bell kneel
by the water's open eyes watering
at her newly conceived counter Eve image, reaching its arms out
pulling her shadow in by the ankles,
the both of them mermaid swimming
mirror married to her source
where the vampire blank had over grown
she was the Willow Queen
of these lost twins banished
from her annulled crowning birth,
now filling in their birth rite positions.

And she, whose name would always mean rebirth,
resurrection in the green algae bearded water
the rugged sure footed Goat boy
in the smiling consummating waves
of the unicorn white night nuptial

## THE BLUE HORSE WIND

floated into each other
merged as Gemini twins;
the blind map hunt
for the illustrious green deer,
their Gemini genesis together,
well spring sprung, begun.

## HER MADNESS (The Dollhouse)

O the torrential tropical
twin tunneling
hurried hurry cane
fury of her madness!
A twister sister of Cane,
radiating radioactive
phosphorescence
from her charged nerves;
keeping her strapped,
zapped jolted,
in electric chair
savoir faire
flair.
Tonight,
when the iron fisted
cruel moon ruler,
steals from the screaming skeleton
keys
their sole fueled purpose,
to unlock the steel sealed passages
of the underground
gleaming rich
cobalt green rock labyrinth.
The metallic satellite
on solitary lock down,
with meteorite beaming
ray gun eyes,
stares glares
at the moody turquoise horses
of the turbulent sea,
on this third planet
rotating
its nemesis rival,
the Medusa flaming snake headed sun;

and out of compacted misery
on the earth it revolver revolves,
compass telltale x-raying
its waxing tidal wave mood
feeds breeds steel steeds
and metallic children,
this warden Punisher
night of denial.

A magnetic receiving tower,
O dark eyed Spanish surrealist woman
whose Freida tropical painted bird mind
wildly spins
a waterwheel,
fluidly stuck
back watering.

As stars stare blades
through the ceiling
of her "red rum" bedroom,
she reads of other Dalhi surrealists,
turns a trick or two
trapped inside this airtight Houdini coffin;
levitates off the sweat soaked bed
elevator elevating
towards the dagger claws
of the Jack the Ripper
 stalker night
you can't out walk,
gripping twisting the lid off
her Frankenstein glowing brain,
"Be patient my Patient," Ha! Ha! Ha!
the psycho psychotic
Jack laughs in mad dog growls.
She grovels, coyote howls
shakes an earthquake,
while the pseudo shrink
Jack, in a foggy Voltaire Candide funk,

shrink shrank shrunk
punked her to thumb size;
a diminished inches
breathing statue,
testimonial to
her insignificance.
Alone, with the teeth kicking,
sword beheading
cutting edge
of the Mien Kempt swaggering night;
She (a skeleton in the closet)
is assisted by another
skeleton in the closet,
Mr. Bones
loans her a hand.
She escapee flees through a crack in the
moaning door,
the hall light overhead is a flying saucer.
She shimmies up the mahogany table leg
on the top of witch stands, estranged
a hushed Victorian oddity
moss adorned Gothic amber doll house.
A shelter from what
creaks creeps and predator growls,
herself, now a Lilliputian
Baby Jane.
She rattles the knob, but the door is jammed,
rap rap Raven rapping,
with tiny knobby knuckles
at the blank face frozen door.
High on the eves,
a lightening forged duplicate
of the Notre Dame fame acclaimed
ribbed wing curved horn gargoyle
chin in hand, squatting
Thinker style; perhaps contemplating
the machinery,
of this inner most dome
he chose

posed to protect;
while silvery skein woven bridal thread
webs, flutter float
anchored in midair.
But no body is there
to answer her, the gargoyle too lofty
to acknowledge
her struggling moth singed wing presence,
his empty sockets staring
past her insignificance,
from his Devil may care
masturbatory shooting glittery stars
perch.

O the foxfire glowing lady,
no dead letter marked
return to sender,
rocks on her hands and knees
an Aries Ram
the first born child of the zodiac,
headbutt rams
the door unstuck, pops open.

By her own invitation,
she slinks into the vacancy,
burglar creaks up the stairs.
O Soledad of Soledad prison,
O Esmerelda
 green emerald woman,
herself a green lantern
through the musty musky dark
she sees no people miniatures,
but a tiny china chihuahua
instead,
comfy in the padded gold chair
squinting its eyes at her,
looking up dazed and confused,
maybe seeking the sombrero hatted sun
spiked cactus and the Tropic of Cancer

border heat
from living past life memories.

What was real before
is not
real now.
What is real
now
is not.

She was no doubt
aware
that the barn red
people furniture house
simply had no back,
left blowing prairie wind wide open,
like the structure
had been
chainsawed in half;
the way the Venus voluptuous assistant
the black funereal coated magician
buzz saws in two,
severing the kicking high heel legs
from the plated vertebrae
at the torso.

Minus piping heat inside,
but rain on the floor
where the shingle chimney less roof
leaked,
(it must have rained in the blue womb room
of the matrix house, pregnant with this mini
red house.)
She spied with her O Esmerelda flashing
emerald eyes,
a teeny weeny box of matches
set by the fireplace,
striking one on her foot
ignited the snoring logs,

then turned her thin fish bone back
sauntering into the linoleum kitchen.
She turned the oven dial to Broil
to kindle some kind of happy warmth,
it glowed incandescently
through the glass window,
like the Hansel and Gretel witch
shoved inside
x-rayed
was disintegrating
evaporating poof!
And then the venomous smoke
began to curl and float
pouring from the fuming gas oven.
Meanwhile pivoting, O Spanish flamenco lady,
distracted from the red flag waving
the riled bull result,
not taking the bull by the horns, as they say,
cowed, utterly
distracted
as she sees O sweet!
a tiny shot glass
with lemon sliced
mini wheel
on the rim,
mini glacial ice cubes (for binocular required
visibility sized polar bears or penguins to
float on ?)
ready maid
waiting for her on the table,
the fire water
of witch
swish,
she downed
drowning.
Suddenly
her face flushed
fever struck,
her braids stood straight up,

141

her widow's peak leaked sweat,
her full house crazy house rage heated up
panic!
From the living room
the fireplace spat
volcanic rolling fire balls,
from the kitchen
the oven seething noxious choking smoke.
Well,
the cow had kicked the lantern
in the shed all right,
and there were no mean green machine
fire trucks to ring,
no phone connected
as the Fire! Fire! Fire! She screamed,
rampaged in waves.
The snapping crackling dollhouse
collapsed
was cremated
on this Black Friday,
and she, the dark eyed Spanish black rose,
stamped her bootless melted foot,
resurrected out of the ashes,
laddering back into
her former size.
That fire forged woman
blew out the last of the smoldering
orange embers
with the force of her Gulliver lungs.
Adios,
moss adorned Gothic home.
Child's chimera house
of make believe,
backless hide out
for the haunted,
panther hunted.

**Poem 2**
O woman of malcontent
the blow fish moon
targets
blowing poison darts
into her necklace of beating hearts,
as she genuflects
pygmy squats
beneath its reflecting alter
creating altered states.
O she of the Frieda passion,
with skin as thin
as a blue paper crane,
who sees with a thousand senses.

O child that never was,
who yowls in heat
when four legged torn ear
battered
pirate fur boot studs
prowl
yowl!
Ride high on storm wrecked fences,
stiff straight lightening rod tails
like penises
as they whisker antenna sniff the air
for female pussy-
cats
in heat.
Like her
of hot chili pepper seasoning.
A sassy orange red pussy cat
who leaves the back door open
for the man in the green
fedora feathered hat,
the whore!

O  pray to the virgin
for this seasonal lady gone astray,
a walking talking
ticking grenade,

as cuckoo as a cuckoo clock
hourly shooting bb pellets
from the o of surprise
in its beaky lips,
every time it mechanically lunges
like its nest is on fire
flung out the popping door.
Alpine
thickly knitted cat eared hat
shoved down over
 its birdy earless ears,
scarf knotted around its scrawny neck
(to hang itself on the hour-
ly hands?)
on sentinel duty, to seize the hour
wrapped in this snowy get up,
during the booming atomic heat raid
mushrooming over
this desert dueling firearm town
of pitch fork Fox news farmers.
O the phosphorescent lady
is shooting the bird, they say.

Save her!
O  starved parched and stabbed
savior of thorns and blood,
nailed to the thousand year cross
for our sins,
flesh and bone son
of the Holy Virgin.

O the villagers dragged her, have you heard?
By her thick rope braids,
she looked like a saint
with that glowing angel face,
but she was a Devil
in disguise,
scratching biting hissing and spitting
like a green eyed Devil possessed witch's cat,
across the open door threshold
of the pristine white steeple church

of our Lord,
when the Catholic bells rang
their swaying headless shoulders sang
an exorcism in Latin,
then cracked, broke in halves.
The violently shaking nina
screamed "O death do not touch me!
Stay back!"
When priest in vacuous black neared,
sprinkled her with holy water
sizzled smoking searing her flesh;
fire leapt from her tongue
Satanically spit
hissing licking
flames creeping up
the cross
the stiff white collared priest
brandished at her.

They tied her hands behind her
shoved her upside down
thumping and kicking
in a sack,
dumped her at the local
loco ward,
strapped her small thrashing body
to the iron bed,
shot her up with something,
her eyes rolled back in her head.
She was just a little kid,
but they were scared of her
thought she possessed powers,
maybe she did,
made her a ward of the ward
being a homeless orphan and all.
She was crafty though,
mapped her escape
for when the distracted staff
was handing out patient dinner trays,
or so the story goes.

143

But they left her alone after that,
she strayed the streets
with feral cats
gave her the pick of the hunt:
mice birds lizards rats,
wiggling catfish
they fisherman snagged from ponds
those little lava eyed tigers,
deftly knocking off
clattering tin lids
like gladiator shields
to do battle with the spears of stars,
pawing through garbage
dragging their reeking find
back to share with that gutter snipe.
Some swear the diamond mind felines
with tiger keen teeth
stabbed pieces of vegetables and fruit,
nourishing treats
just for that animal girl
itching with lice and fleas.

Cleaned and groomed her hair to shining
with pink sand papery tongues
like they done to their own young uns',
so is she
without doubt
part cat.
I must admit
those outlaw cats
with squirming swarms of kittens
at their swollen teats,
did better for her
then those church goers did,
fur sure.

O what a shocking history
this story of the muchacha
whose mournful yowls

cause the proud
Medusa fire snake sun
to fall down
drown in its own river of blood.

O this sister of Cane
who steals sugar cane
from yielding fields,
her teeth,
like little white glittering
sugar cubes.
Who eats red hot chili peppers
a small dragon exhaling fire
that licks the stars,
ignites the rooster gold sun to rise.
Whose electric whirling energy
prickles needles down your spine,
tattoos Satan, on pristine breasts of seraphim,
smoking their white feathers black.

Warrior woman
a painted animalist
who lifts the dead eye gaping fish
off ice chips in the markets,
turns to cross
the pebbly beach,
tosses lunar scaled fish
back into the pearl mother sea;
where
breathing the water in gulps
organs regenerate
and Ophelia revived,
the smiling fish
stand on their heads
waving tails
in swaying salute,
dive deep beneath
where maroon algae gardens grow
in a peaceful coral village
beneath the moody Titan sea.

She who swings open
cage doors,
so nightingale avian
sing, even in freezing downpours,
sail in gales to turquoise feathery trees.

She an armed tree of fire
spits bullets
at cruel en slavers,
splits in half
with rage,
and then is made whole
at the the turn of the tides.

Whose caterpillar vision
is as myopic
as a cyclops.
Beneath her flesh
animal fetus ripple,
her melon green breasts
swell with milk,
her raven hair
strung in bell ropes
chimes to the ground,
inviting color morphing chameleons
to swing from verdant vines
climb up her ropes,
king of the mountain sit
on top of her indigo head
dragon hiss,
swing back and forth
between
her smooth braids
and the twining vines.

O
radiation lady
radiating green,
roaming the sphinx riddled catacombs

of the emperor night,
where it rains
pouring salt
over wounds

the desiccated mask
of the painted desert,
its sunken eye holes
through witch
its blistering sand eyes
hallucinate
a plush green parrot
oasis
with rushing waterfalls;
not this barren parched
tight lipped and cracked,
humped (carrying its own cistern of water)
camel toe messenger,
dry to the bone drama
where everything shrivels and shrinks
on the brink of madness.

O foxfire glowing lady
who on black cougar
haunted
hunting nights,
can lose her strut,
sink into a quicksand sinkhole
reduced to Lilliputian size,
that shrinking woman
O Soledad,
chained by a skinny ankle
to the metallic
lock down moon.

# THE GOURD

With her transparent pollinated petal fingers, she rolled in her pale orange pearl, footloose beginnings; the genesis origin of her cosmic squash species. Her later Libra scaled balance or unbalance, suspense-fully scale suspended, tilting swinging uncertainly now, as she neophyte burst forth on her sanguine gold child wrapped in blue clouds, weather zone climate dependent, climax ending in health and volume wealth journey. Thus tilting the weighing scales, as an elephantine size, Janus double faced globe; tiny ants with antenna compass, would sail across on diminutive legs, amazed. This was the painted lady butterfly, black and orange patterned, undulating winged insect fairy god mother, gilded pollen sprinkling from sheer membrane wings, Blessing. Ushered forth purely, with no portends of a star crossed seed besieged with ill omens. For who would wish such a merciless venal malignancy, stabbing the needle in the third eye, blinding the  faith of the orange pearl spherical infant.

Not that one is naive to the world of black veiled widows, hardcore porno sadistic murderess in transparent negliges, funeral thread spun. Wearing sheer black stockings, thorax throbbing, dominatrix brandishing eight secreted black spun whips; to beat the lust hypnotized memorized, tied up bonded Aztecan sacrificial satiating partner. Her sea of eyes chosen He, who ejaculates into his Caligula mate, hundreds of arachnid eggs, his hairy heirs inheriting his ancestral ancient tribunal tribal chromosomes and traditions. Thus dubbed guiltless, by her ancient female fang sating brain. Theater Snuff movie commencing, finishing her sex act, the self actualized almost widow, No Mercy, Kill Bill driven, while her mate's galvanized eight eyes, mirror reflect the red violin hidden on her belly, helplessly staring at her hateful, but tasteful (to her) crime. Never had he serviced such a flaming searing ecstatically erotic organism before, as this was his first and only untimely time. Completing her rite of passage ritual, into her self absorbed widowhood, eating him alive, until riven piece by piece, her fangs draining the dregs.

Then Caligula mad, she sensitively plays, though ear less and tone deaf,the red violin, dripping the instrumental  poison, into her next vexed web chosen fly by customer. Who is not privy to her Dominex Matrix Madam, Jackie the Ripper, sado masochistic, exclusively sex shared bonds. Is simply a preferred orderb.

Yet this was the celebration of the, though non celibate in conception, flower delivered Nazarene rounded stemming baby. Not a scorpion stinging invitation, to be contemplating such appalling,without even a respectful pall bearing coffin funeral- Evils.

Much later, (though one must take into accord,the brief, quick, fleeting on mercurial winged feet, temporal gourd, much later, being the cloaked in green Spring, to pomegranate ruby cheeked clover sweet summer) yielding a  discordant umbilical corded gourd. Bathed rayed, deep dye cast by the Madonna starlit sun, on her circus beyond giant, endlessly tall giraffe neck stilts, meridian high rose garden prismatic shades, daily secular tour of duty. A religious non religious exhilarating, tinfoil tanning room, aureate after a storm, Madonna adagio reliquary. Though indeed the horse phallus Pan Goat, Bestiality conceived God, walking erect on his two cloven hoof legs, (whose reputation for angel receiving, maiden head, tipsy maidens, rivaled Jupiter's) was present, present. Tipping glossy silky ears sideways, to hear the needs of the vegetable color colony, juicy fruit children (especially the ripe mega purple grapes, along with the carnival starlet sun). As part of his tender tinder box love potions, palisades staked. Pan the keeper, not to be fleeced of his Nepenthe ambiance, debauchery infectious fever, swilling supply, by any of the foxy crafty, tailed nibblers.

Entering again the galloping gamut, of the pale orange pearl; tongue swirling, magicus onyx odyssey, of the omega vine rooted girl.
As early on, True blue to her dramatic easily bruised, high strung congenital female throbbing genitals. Jumping overboard, off the beaten path, unseasoned thyme unrhymed reasoning, being just short of a seedling. The trauma bee stinging, allerically alert, stem gored gourd, squashed by Peter Peter Pumpkin Eater fears; leaving a seedy pith pit, where an electric blue werewolf, five pointed red pentagram in hairy palms fit.
The umbra beclouded country bumpkin, ultra sonic visual kinetic electric werewolf injected, keen though tilted perceptions, detective detections. Equaling hundreds of revolving N. S. E. W. spinning eyes, speaker receiving pairs of caterpillar row lined ears. An explosion of piano playing touch tone fingers, attached to hands down pressing against the non stop drumming ground sound. Symphonic cacophonic senses feeding her feasting globular meridians on overload. Lessening the horizontal margin between dread and revered awe at what she saw, until she was consumed . Short sighted fear incited, targeted by a rain of impaling nails. Psychological trepidations of course, so her pumpkin rhyming rind was not hurt.

It was not her Just Deserts,
left shaking in her boots, spinal vine cord shivering at the sundering thundering
four dark horses of the apocalypse, child projected entrance, of a Gracula winged Dracula ominous potent, though impermanent, unless shuttling through the No Where Lands of outer space; Dark Lord stopped clock black hole blind sight. Voldemort nose less night; denying her of her honey gilded golden girl liquid formula, vitamin diet, Vatican slanted angular light teat nourishment.
    In spite of it, she tolled cadmium sulfide bright orange tree orange. The orange so generator generating, recondite, nuclear novel adamantly clamant, annulling any other orange. So under the solar exploding with geometrical conical cylinder shapes, yellow yellow bathroom window, the pond goldfish in the back lot, paled in comparison. Not that the amber amour mail scaled nervous bubble eye fish noticed, too busy warring over who stole the next winking puckering red orange, undinal mermaid tailed kiss, from the next pretending to resist, cosmic orange lady fish in waiting.
    But in ass backwards hindsight, most of the hosting neighbor hood (that later gave up the ghost of belief), the purple tinged furry moles of the underground subway lamp less drilling miners,

minus hard hats (are the shoveling dirt critters really blind, or is that a Jehovah mouth spread myth, because their tiny pin prick eyes, blink shut when they meet the cyclops fury of the colossal celestial eye?)

Wily guileful bandana pirate, carrots and red leafy wreathe lettuces, from the coffin shaped growing green boxes. Yanking treats by tasty fibril roots, down down into their subterranean, fossorial gloved front feet, hands down achieved, tubular linking labyrinths. Earth walled dug outs, futuristically, science fictionally, ahead of their current actions, down the cabal line, to permit turnstile passage of toy size subway electricity lighted window magic cars.

Flashing past to the next tunneling garden rich, peeking underground potatoes, vacant tenant neighborhood, stepping off or whizzing onward over curving breathless tracks.

Plus the aged wing die hard fading moths, and the flat fat body curling stripy stinkbugs, stigmatized by their lingering skunky stink, had long believed, in their weak summer insectile inter wishing, intersecting of failing flight fight, revolving glass door ride. The moth co. that is, and the other back lot pansy faced, star mole personnas, that Felicia, so named by her avian cageless mother (besides the Madonna stilts tilted scarlet starlet sun). To be wed, as the gored stem gourds' ordained, baptized by a zealous wind drifting lifting pollen name; equating happiness in a different tongue. (Not really suiting her segmented beclouded nature, perhaps in hopes of reforming it.) Her signature title signed by presiding residing raccoon spoor.

This Sublime pumpkin girl, would be hailed as the Holy Grail, perfect rind flesh and impeccably raised (away from the calcified bone thick lips of pecking pock marking birds). Naturally excluding, her sparrow gray mocking bird mother, who dive bombing tries, to safe guard, preserves, her daughter's paramont, cherub rounded beauty. (This vocal caurosel, who will soon be well met, as we put a spin on our travelling merry-go-round.) Entitling Felicity (her unnicked, candle wick nick name) to the winning title of: "The Glazed Orange Lip Kissing Gala Gourd Provincial Princess." This local contest fizzy orange soda pop co. supported. Serving a free gushing orange splurge during the comparative high and ebbing hours.

The pride and joy of her animal, imago, amphibious neighbors (but not the melarky hierachy goldfish, who can't bubble beyond their water world intrigue). Felicity's, (using the name known only to close intimates) thick harvest walled uterus, Wish Hope and Dream, blessed fecund as the white black blizzard dotted spotted blonde dandelion fur, pregnant with unbreakable color abundant Easter eggs. Brake less March hare wild eyed, cloud scut, rapid heart thumping, jumping out of the delicate rib clad vested chests, in a blink flash rabbits. Swollen heavy laden with tear shaped seeds, germinating more Cinderella Coach, field mice shape shifting. All in the back lot being familial familiar with the puff magic Sanskrit script, having gotten a whiff of the Fairy Tail inscribed, ancient broken back Grimm book. The towering stair children with pussy willow soft, electric spring blue eyes, read to each other, out side when creatures spider hide. Where the random field mice metamorphosed, into a motor charged horse powered team. (So the belittled little crumb seekers, sneaking on dainty pink ballerina feet, brown earth eyed, an augmented august August pollen dusted crop of mice, dreamed that they too be transformed, born again as lucky horse shoe hoof huge earth quake trembling. Clysdale Milk wagon clinking bottle, colossal galactic Milky Way Galaxy horses. A heavenly eidolon chosen, equestrian high stepping tail braided brigade parade. Barouche coach esquiring, a sun aspiring, pompous pumped plump pumpkin. In drag, if predestined by the carnival administering kaleidoscopic fates, to be a thick skinned male, dressed like a queen, pumpkin drawing team.

Yet plague sore blighted, as the best laid oviparous pouring forth plans gone puss rotten. Most of the gauged for, stamen pistil whipped dreams, of the back lot element, for the plum cheeked visionary pumpkin, deflated with a tired going flat tire hissss. When a mid evil ill omen, cholera over flowing, sewer ugly river of hag harpy ogress huge bumpity witch wort lumps, froze on Felicia's glamor girl magazine, model flawless fresh flesh of undreamed features. So the naively once believed, sewn up pumpkin beauty contest, was canned.

The north and south, Janus two faced, as both sides decidedly could be carved, frost clinging gourd, had, after all, been prostituted by the back lot's high priestess ambitions for her. Now, no longer a smash hit, with the cabbage patch, pull the cell sexed baby up by its goblin green hair, rotor mole rotating neighborhood. Cursed worse, the cry baby multi-eyed potatoes, undamned damning tears, flooded the back lot, up to the moaning steps of the giant's laddering staircase to the hazy tearing stars.

The bug eyed flooded grave plant tenants, on their last leg, flower phoned, a Cassandra Reverse Magic maji. Backwards paddling, wrinkly wizened hard shell, duck tuck and hide, red eared slider shrink. Sporting waterproof wrap around glasses, on his bridgeless nose, above the powerful beak. He exorcist appeared, chanting in pig Latin Z-A incantations, at last delivering the stormy teary water, back back to the river giver, before everyone caught leprosy, molded shrunk, defunked.

O the opiate poppy seed dreaming laureate aureate laudamus days of wine, from the swollen to bursting glory grapes, and the carillan thick honey comb sweet cell buzzing ambrosia of the drunk and generous Pan pundit Gods was over.

Though the beetle juice occupants, microscopically studied the sun setting big bang theories of why? Felicia's Oz ma, blotted blotched Magnolia demise.

**Part two**

It was painfully plain, as the un carved noses, on her carnival orange, engorged stem gourd. Eidolon secret eyes, curtained behind the rind, faceless future faces. Crystal gazer poltergist lucid, spawned before the acrimonious, cholera sewer spread plague, left its ugly giantess ogress, Friday the 13th bumpity crop of sordid witch worts. That Felicia grim reaper, Medusa snake froze. Bogey bomb qualmed at the heart stopping rise, of the 3rd Reich inflexible stiff leg booted gait. Entrance of the breath taking, incubus succubus, nose less Voldemort, usurping night. But this was due to her 24-7 on sentinel duty, conceived in her pithy pit, electricity biting, spine tingling werewolf.
Many other compadres received the Lotus Eater twilight, with leafy, thorny, furry, or lizard

camoflauged amiable arms, (weather twiggy or thick) wide open, unalarmed. Breathing in the unmasked blooming, forgetful fumes, of the Nepenthe etherizing, deep black silk cat night. All said and done, undone under this inviting, inviolable, swarthy furred purring blanket. Being the other half of the Janus two faces, simultaneously looking past backwards, future forward, whirling twirling sibilant blue planet's orbiting day.

But Felicia, Felicity, the iron irony of her names! Seige beseiged, with nightmare dashing out her own brains, infant suicidal driven visions; before she had given up pleasure sucking, on the swirling with pumpkin milk umbilicus. Both when her despotic psychotic night sweating terror, of a grim cinder snowing, high boot flooding despot, of the impending non bending knee patrol, was present and not present. He was omnipresent, stemming out from beyond the stem rim. Stimulated by her assimulated paranormal paranoia, 45 magnum Big Bang! firing off these delusional illusions. O the enigmatic mysteries, under the stem hat, helter skelter lodging, in the brain's gooey ectoplasmic drooling, haunted bone house! How rude of me here, for so fecklessly meditating on the incarnate bone cavern. Not reckoning, in Felicity's case, the gooey seedy stringy orange fiberous, ectoplasmic drooling, haunted rime rind house. Please forgive me.

Another high blood pressure, added factor, boiling crucible, scorpion stinging tail spell, pepper tickling the monsoon sneeze of boils. Angst double hammered, by a blood red consuming electric Jesus, wearing the bare bodkin stabbing crown, gruesomely nailed to a cross. This diswrought pulsant obtrusive image, inflated, folded; kindled again in a flickering, color candle shrine, within her gory glory religious warring mind.

At a nursery rocking horse time, when Mother Goose in triangular teepee top, visor rim brim, burnished buckle hat, should be rocketing on her convoying employed, honky, puffy pillowy feathered, wander lust, stick horse necked goose. Ungracefully chased, by a daisy ruminating, smiling purple muzzle, non cowering, brown sugar spotted, tailing cow. Rump hoofs kicking, knicking silver spoon moon, as the milk nozzled, Daisy woven diadem, undaunted bovine supreme ly jumped. The same in duplicate, fat spoon moon, as the octopus hatted bell jingling clamant minstrel, galvanized toddler, bangs on his over sized Humpty Dumpty head, wobbling dangerously on pinky finger sized neck. Potato sack slumped in his highness throne. Only the satellite spoon, magnetized by the sonic ears flight of light years, that are hundreds of years from beaming the colossal spoon. The cadmium sulfide girl neglected, unable to reflect on these cereal milky magics—

For Poor, open door Felicia, raked over angry, smouldering red coals, reaper raped with disturbia, virus ridden forbidden religious affairs. Her pickett fence teeth, kicked in, due to a vile theurgy nozzled trespasser, forcing himself upon her. Giving her virulent phantom vision, of the zealous over cooked, uncouth rude dog, falsely sainted Borges Pope. Papal embedded, in a Babylonian carved, Snow White rippling canopy bed. Engraved with stern lipped, cavern eyed, purity hospital smocked, hissing goose winged angels. Roundure creased, corpulent thighed and dimpled buttocks, ogling goggle eyed, flitting cupid bow lipped kissing cherubs. In village size snowy satin sheeted empire, pillows freshly fluffed with plucked goosing feathers. The debauchery layered bed flocked with incestuous breeding half witted sisters, brothers, sons daughters. Hair crimping girdle imprisoning maids of wives. No one was denied, though Tom Bedlam mad cap clap, shuffling gaited syphilis, dripped like a puss leaky faucet.

These conflicting seedy scenes, stuffed within the pulpy layers of the untempered babe's Trinity – in flaming white satin, (the holy ghost draped in vapours) – verses the rise of the black hearted 3$^{rd}$ Reich night. Mainly the strain on her brain, over two squirming views, too confusing reigns, of whose is dove love sacred, and whose is Devil food's cake.

So again she was impaled by the crucifix driven nails rain. Ohhh! Her poor squashed head. Adding further binocular insight, to clarify, the branched dividian divide.

(Sadly, the mortician ripening mortification, sower sewn into the fruit and vegetable children's fontanel vulnerable, tissue layered viable heads, by the false wired hand, of the hired handy man.)

The other youngsters shrugged it off their global rounded shoulders. However, with Felicity's electrified, fried and gullible,quick silver hallucinagenic, thin skin nature (though her rind was thick). Sorely indeed, she was in need of an exorcism from the conception of sin. As the hard core, born again, tough skin zealous extra taught. She was wrought with the sin of being pistil shot into the stamen, creating her sinful seed. Plus the snake forked tongue conjunctions of the Anaconda crushing Borges scandalous scenery. (The planter man, in green jeans, a rehearsed perverse pervert! Cause and effect, popping button eyes, due to his shoe tied too tight, biblical tainted restraints. Peeking Tom obsessed was he, with sexual antics, unpeeled revealed, under the organs still saluting, smacking of holy smocks.)

Why the idea of that seedy hired man, impregnating the little sprouts and root children with his sexual barage, filthy garage of filmy "religious erotocism," just makes one possessed, puke to purify!

And Because Felicia alone, shrine kindled the electric though unplugged Jesus, split level housing the omnipotent Voldemort noseless Nazi night. The finger stuck in electric socket, hair on back of neck standing up bristling blue werewolf. His hairy hands tinkering, cross wiring, showers of sparks electrocuting her interactive reactors. Bravely, though nearsightedly, she held the shaken snow globe, of hell and brimming hailstones. Damnation, flying scarlet devil tailed night mares, with herself standing in the black snowing middle, inside, until it was too late!

In jury defense, of the blind leading the blind, relative friends—

No one knew, to flower phone, the rhyming mottled scales, horny dome home, but soft hearted exposed parts, Reverse Magic expert, turtle ducking tucking shrink. If ignorance were cited as no excuse, than those who purportedly poured acid into their own eyes, resolute blinded; could be junctioned, edict perjured, tribunal Franco shot. As an uncommon courtesy, black bandana tied around their already sightless eyes. Mercy percieved as weakness, the deadly deed, smoking gun, Franco style trigger finger, chamber executed. Not that we would wish for such dire rifle firing, even rubber bullets, aimed at our heedless gentian frivolous friends; for their lack of sighted insight. Besides, we are all guilty of being daft drafted, short sighted, and our unfiled shot and piling corpses, would pack a pedestrian thread bare writhen city sized tumulus.

Like the ragged brusque shallow mass Indian burial grounds, the later crypt enshrined padres, had the totemic halcyon people, dig out with rocks, for their own upcoming self departures.Beasts! Those heads stuck up their ass, leathery mummified heart savage priests!

If her guileless neighboring back lot citizens, some salamander quick, 911 alerted the red ear slider, lettuce guerdoned expert. His spiked claw flat paws, andantes waving, as he chanting cantus priest, exorcise exported, sanctioned her drowning toxic sea of puke green troubles, to torrent current backwater. Evaporate from the cadmium orange pithy virgin fruit cavern Thus fugue clouding, leaving no vestige, intersecting heirloom, of the agonizing apotheosis compulsions, bad Vlad spike impaling her.

Horned as the horned moon, angora sweater furred Pan, might have liberated Felicity, from the monastic ropes binding her, stern lip rubbing, banefully cutting her bleeding juice wrists. Pouring sips of his Nepenthe pacifying foot loose wine, into her segmented orange glow lips. If he had given her more hocus pocus focus, abolishing her polished shame. All in vain, Billy goat thumping on his split hooves, tail wagging, tagging after split tail maiden heads, through the assuaging, unrepenting carnal satyriasis stirred vermeil season forest. As that is the written in stone way of artifice grape trafficking, nodding goateed satyrs.

Yet blame is useless, dead weight. Not that the blowing his own horn Goat Man, would turn himself into a scapegoat. Stilted guilt, not part of his cloven hoofs, stomping grapes into sooo ruby or deep indigo wine swilling. Horned moon, driad trees holding up the sky with scarlett leafy dressed gnarly fingers, fuzzy caterpillars climbing bark in green boots, light footed or clomping, dissolute stomping grounds.

And there were other crucible, bubbling to the boiling point, boiling over, smoky braid twists. Disturbia sister blistering, eminent to the volanic eruption of the rotten goose egg boils, ribbeting toad witch worts. Ah! there's the rub, spotting puss rows on her complex complexion.
The cattle prodding, electric fence incidents, hidden until  map searched. Hecate forks in the road, sophist sword pointed, sextant marges to measure. Sooo, here we enter the portal of the ornately ornamental glass menagerie. A too frangible intangible zoo, mirror housing a wind chiming chimeric unicorn. Its bee stinger, salve third eye sylph catharsis, humming bird needle pointed, thorn pricking horn, thin and transparent as a ghost.

Sliver stalled with the unicorn, a silent lion roaring griffin, with air singeing singing wings, unchained by gravity. A Pegasus, with ankles so slight, they winked with dawn's brinking corona blink. And a reindeer with rain skin, sirroco fanning river branching rippling antlers. This glass citadel zoo, fabricated in good fairy mosaic pattern butterfly faith, by her salient sailing, plain ear less, sparrow gray mocking bird fostering mother, constant as the sun. This winsome Wendy bird, perched on the roof of her grass feather, tufts of fur, mint leaf aromatic, straw woven, wild sweet strawberry fluorescent home. From the orphic revealing moment, drawn to the orange pearl infant's orphaned delivery. Wind squired, delivering the fattest early bird worm, prize offered to Felicity's segmented orange glow lips. (Most likely the grubbing dirt swallowed the worm eating, digesting incongruous chips in the soil, smoothing it out around Felicia. Over the pink, pooping out smooth humus, digesting ingested sand grains, minute rocks.)

This kalidiscopic black bead eyed, airy avian, bonded with her emerald green grass woven blanketed, teal bootied, stem headed, mittened daughter, more than some mothers of the human flesh! The aviary pilot, a gray night light, patient singing sentry sentinal.

Her umbra blurred, but Tropical color bird, vibrating throat, hundred tongued river branching mother, sang to her precious intuitive daughter, of her most beloved encounters. Memorizing the mesmerizing, shell grooved, replenishing songs about geese with pumpkin orange beaming gourd moons on their wings. Of unnamed animal, natural decomposing in the earth, necropolis grounds. Recognized by a phosphorous serenity, embryonic hovering glows, waiting to be uterus implanted, transplanted into the three dimensional, trembling thirsty lipped, rooted terrestrial again.

Of blue purple green houses on stilts, the silver skein river wish fish, that help to hold up the water world, by their gauntlet ed fin hands, swam swim under. Of smooth blue bibbling pebbles, stacking themselves, for the shape shifting river, to fluid little river horse leap over. Of purple moles with green moon eyes, quivering shivering green bud souls, exodus exiting on pink soles, the moody damp lamp - less gloomy wormy wormwood underground. Diving board springing into a dandelion twirling, blowing fluff wishes united, in Peace, felicity forecast. (Like that woods would ever happen!)

So Felicity, unhappy hapless daughter of the sparrow gray, regally giving, interpreter, integral diapson singer of a convivial blended cantos. Keeper kept in a chimera blown glass castle (don't forget the road to Hell is paved with good intentions). Spirited away from those who smash pumpkins, laugh at their seedy brain mess. Yet the frangibility of the glass walls, so easily fractured, and the too fright night vulnerable glass menagerie; Ah! Cheri, further enhanced accentuated, mirror reflected the pumpkin girl's own mental frailties. Circus ride sliding, tilting the unbalanced Libra scale balance,down down to the crystal stalagtite horned, Boreal south pole. This would be a thorn in the heart, of her radiant melodizing humming bird pollinating mother, forever—witch is sadly never ever lasting, in any fruit vegetable (unless preserved in preserves, witch to human flesh is like being frozen in spacial timelessness, dead) or organ beating fleeting species.

Felicia, dye in the wool cast, would she end up like the once beloved, executioner axed, in front of her titan towering but helpless integral family, inertia stuck by their deeply rooted feet. Dragged from the anchorite powdery snow angel winged illimitable fortress of her familial derivation. Photosynthesis expectancy lasting (without human infernal intervention) for eons. The brief piny skirted, dainty furry Little Fur Tree; stuffed in an attic like an unwanted corpse. This the cruel grueling recourse, after her boughs decked, with welcoming home waxing flame wick candles. Cranberry and buttery popcorn chains, bubble shaped wish eye reflecting ornaments. Like a decorated soldier stripped of his badges, the little fur tree stripped of her babbles, trinkets, the tasty Christmas chains, eaten by sharp ivory forests, of glinting enamel mammal chompers.

A mere shadow of herself, she lay wasting away in the mole like dark, dropping her pine scented, now brown needles, one at a time, exposing her bare knobby spine.

O the celebrating revelers can be so blind, so unkind. Golden roasted turkeys, turned on the spit, dressed in dressing, a festive feast fit for Gods. After the Roman food orgy, the turkey's carcass mercilessly tossed to mange balding menacing hackles dogs.

O would Felicity be just another unjust star crossed tragedy? Daughter of the, well yes, overly shielding, swelling breasted, rainbow vibrant, vibrating perfect pitch, hemp woods housed, hundred tongued, fluidly fluent mocking bird.

Sagaciously courted by providence, kismet kissed by Phoebe's pale lips, her eidolon ethereal slender beam finger pointing, at the hoar frosted pumpkin girl. Marking her for an ample, conciliatory concerted change. At the following rise of the sunglasses shielded Madonna, strutting on the taller than any country spotted giraffe neck, stilts laddering beyond beyond. The boy and girl giants, with pussy willow soft, deep as digging a hole to China Blue eyes. Like long legged spirited blue colts, thundering down the staircase leading to the stars, when traveling back up. "O children are divine, they skip rhyme past the defined, shiny pebbles skipping over the murky muddy old river." The amber braided girl in jeans, a pirate, brandishing jack knife, "O let us cut her loose now, the one we watched and waited for, grow salient from a flower."

The calyx children clapped, did not turn putrescent faces away, at Felicity's ogress bumps. Slicing a circular circumference, around her stem hat, pulled it off. Spoon scooping out the pulpy city of seeds, some sank into the holy dirt, fomenting her children's crop to crop up. Allowing her communing harmonious tongued mother, to evolve into a grandmother.

Then with patient, patient focus, the knife wielding surgeon, sliced through Felicity's rind, a thrall faced revengeful Calibus, Caligula on the war path mask. Trading off the brow sweating gambado, full swing job, with her gusto little brother. He more than accurately cutting, a bride of Frankenstein scarred face, north of south, behind the mad Caligula howling. Completing Felicity's strange competing, Two faced global range.

Do you believe these hack saw jack knifed savageries, tragedies? O but the brilliant kids, wise, unlatching, A Blessing in disguise. The timid Quaker quaking, rain of nails impaled, bride of vulture tearing tortures, now vaunting flaunting a Craken waking Monster, parting the seas storming face. Plus the missing, lightening seared, generated, risen mate, of the isolated long suffering, though vengance driven dangerous. Ghoulish dead skin patched, man hatched Frankenstein. These chattering chattels, christened rebellious rebirths, hers. Erasing her night sweating crucifix stabbing, dressed in pristine white silky sheets, Borges charging, the Vladimort noseless nights! of holy eternal conflict. Fugue and blush, brushed away, away! Along with the bristling paw taunting, electric blue Beware, werewolf, Gone!

This the birthday of Felicity's transformation proclamation. Twin candles galloping inside her gallant dragon toothed, triangular and cresent eyed fierce, but welcoming fearless double face presence. "The Best Pumpkin King ever!" For Kings are Queens and Queens are Kings. "Hurrah!"

Praised the elated kids. Fervently Felicity's images shrine levin in their waking Craken, Frankenstein bride zombie, wide mirroring eyes.

Post is the after math, when the ghost of Halloween, shivering in the breath smoking cold, wails its post partum blues, at the bed ridden, hidden under dark cloud covers, pale thin bones of light. One might believe concieve this to be, the bloody November, funeral demise, of a golden orange, lapis lazuli wistful wisteria, country natal, young pumpkin girl. Smashed, cracked up, carted away in the Bedlam garbage truck, to a rotten exile, at the steeping seeping sotweed dump.

Shrink shrank shrunk, contaminated by beggarly leprosy, her sericeous toes and legs, subterfuge filtering chord attuned fingers, eaten away to stumps. The gangrene green tarantula hairy mould fungus, poison dotted mottled disease, squashing all her faith, candle knighted confidence, seized. Rat devoured, her so briefly encountered, Candle Lite Savings time, high lighted hours.

But let us not cave in, losing perpetually blooming catus flowering hope. As the now rueful back yard lot; dumping Felicity, soon as the ogress, spell boiling witch worts, tatooed their trail of tears. Wending down her once smooth, macrocosmic, north and south pulsing, virgin curtained faces. Soon as her feet no longer fit, into their rubbery garden booted, pomp routed, scheming Orange Soda Beauty Queen dreams. Beggardly, their eyes spooned out, dead fish blind to the fact, the friends since Felicity's orange pearl birth; pimping this gifted with heightened sensory girl. The below the stairs banjo twanging lot, unwittingly stupified, collectively collecting Fool's Gold.

Yet forgiveness is bountiful, for the lettuce handkerchief people, whose cosmic understanding of the intangible is nebulous.

And each evil twin, bad seed deed, germinates a praise worthy one, in the Libra scaled, high tight rope wire cirque, Yin Yang balancing act. The Art of Reverse Magic, capable of canceling out a catastrophe. Brobdingnagian moving mountains, back to their sloping space, beneath the piercing chins of crepuscular star people.

And Felicity, at last, relieved of the hairy monkeys, acrobatically stacked furry simian pyramid, weighted on her back. After basking in the Gargoyle sainted, galvanized glory, of a candy gory Halloween. Gifted with offerings of (dipped in Dorothy's melted sparky red shoes) candy glimmering apples. Chocolate caramel coconut fluff in shiny tinfoil wrappers, stuffed and fattened like a Cannibal Queen! Inebriated sated, by the licorice wafting, bats ascending from the campaniles, hallowed Halloween, gratuitously ingested, digested. A candle in her uterus struck, flaring tear drop switching on, her Craken heightening roar. And on the back of front, her Frankenstein stitched bride, lighthouse beaming, flashing "I'm here, you're long, so late awaited" at her somewhere lost fated matching mate.

O far too brief, Felicity's embellished relished orange tabernacle, of candy cannibal doubly faced jubilant focus, ended with a hissss! Magic thumb, tongue wet pointer finger, flicking out the wick. A ghost of smoke, Ouch! The levin gone too quick! O these envisage memories, an orange poppy field of fortune smiling lips, never to cede, recede, from Felicity's consciousness.

When all was said and done, undone by the witch threaded, silver tinseled, diaphanous hands of the skein weaving scarfed, frost breathing, blue bowler hatted twilight.

Avast! Lo, looky over yonder! At the pumpkin people akimbo, waiting in orange limbo, tangerine rindy folks, whose levin festival house, eyes nose and mouth, candle less blacked out. Those still standing survivors, who had not been smashed, preserved in preserves, baked into a gourd die pie. Called to Felicity twice, in a recondite, fallen stipple leaf wormwood waning dried husk voice. "Come come, let us dice roll away!" Felicia, Felix part of the receptive, interceptive, confluence purple umbra hatted crew. Galvanizing the crafted, pumpkin ship, with swarthy, trumpeting sainted pirate skull escorting bat wing raggedy sails. Slipping into fissuring crevices, swallowed up by earth's cracked lips. The antiphonal crew, lunging, plunging down chutes, like the shooting chute to the laundry cage. Then spring ejected by the ship, dangling fibril arms and legs, wrapped around oblong circular pumpkins spinning, circling. Down down into the green, velvety moss plush sofa center. Guerdoned with chocolate treats, yellow and orange striped candy corns, red candy dollars. Flowing orange soda bicarbonate glowing, for these replenishing, hollering giggling guests, resounding medicinal consanguineous toasts. Served by xylophone ribbed skeletons, hosted by vaporous ghosts.

Taking a black sabbath sabbatical, league of brief curling tongue leaves, leave of microcosmic, orange occult absence. Of haloed nightmares, orange mare streaking roof leaping phantoms. Stabled until the next grave Halloween, All Saints Hallowmas. When the quixotic, fire cat pupiled pumpkin people, preserved by the mossy couch crouching vacuum (along with the chiming, or vaporous hosts) spin, load the calender charted, skull and cross boned, black mass flagging pirate ship. Skating back through worm holes in time.

When the frost is orange on the gourds, and our winning pumpkin girl, holds the key to felicity, in her twining vine rope, five pointed star leaf, autumn script furling mitt.

# LEONARDO'S DREAM SEED

The stardust
Twilight
Furred
Wherewolf,

From zero invisibility
Into the solid Z.

Lightning zigzagged
Sizzled clapped
Over his perked pricked ears
As he Steppenwolf
Stair stepped
Into this snuffed
Wick-
ed
Present
Of cannibal devoured
Presents.

Where
moon scaled
Celestial swimming
Pisces wish fish,
Dracula
Impaled on thorn horned spears,
Oozed yellow globby gelatinous
shimmering star blood
Across a snuff movie
backdrop
Silent screaming rabbit trap
bedeviled by the scent
Of singed fur.
The sheeny gluey
gooey
Ectoplasmic leaking stars

Sticking to the paws or feet of whatever dared creep.
And though pygmy spotted frogs
lapped at the star juice,
Uncurling unfurling glowing tongues
Faintly
Firefly
Flickering
Against the lidless
Gray mask.

The stardust
dusk dusted
Where wolf,
Frozen in woe
For the woe-be-gone,
Paused with paw lifted
Sniffing
"Where art mine?"
Blood tears smeared
Across his muzzle mask.
Ears flat
Against his head
Back
Howling
At the funereal
Les miserable
Smoky plague.
Through this purgatory
Theater of the damned
bone snapped
Gory territory,
Ragged
Bat winged seraphim
Using sonar
Flitted across fallen trees
Like rows of wooden soldiers
That hit the dirt,
These pregnant Alien angels

Escorted transported
totem animal spirits
Wrapped flashing in their jellyfish
transparency
Into other black hole dimensions.

But in this cursed
And shriveled heart,
Baneful painful
Woods,
Scattered in
Broken wrist arm and shoulder boughs,
Nests
Deftly woven with flower garlands
Of hair, feathers
Fallen willow leaves
Laced with string and straw,
Lovingly beak picked
For the now
Cradle cracked eggs.
The dried up fetus
Still clinging
Inside
Split ceiling
Fracture fragile
rift globes.

Oh what broken wing
Dead zone
Hiroshima
Sin,
Had the blue wolf
With midnight sun
pirate ship
Billowing wings
pirating away,
caustically caused
by abandoning the global bubble
Of this chameleon eye popping

Arcadia.
Believing himself
Ina universe
Parallel
To his pearl
Paragon,
Oyster
Inviolable.

For the bleu veined wherewolf
Drained by the weighted
Mermaid breasted
Guardian ship,
Had backwatered,
Sailing against
The lashing sea of time
To his timeless origin.

Craving rejuvenation
In the marrow nurturing sorcery
Of his floating feather dream
Beginning.
The wolf
Reentered
the gobliness
white moon furred
sloping
with the shared weight of his sibs,
lumpy rippling
belly
of Wolvina,
his unbridled
bride of the full moon
its unwinding bridal train
howling,
matrix.
Tunneling through her uterus
She bona fide
bore him

As a pup again
(along with his bone marrow sibs)
Umbilical anew.
She expertly chewed
To sever him
As a complete being,
Being complete.
Nuzzling against her warm magenta teats
Healing sealing his old wounds,
Sucking the genial genius
Of his genesis,
guzzling her blue milky way
fostering elixir.

Then
Inspired with the rebirth
Of the primal survival fire bud
Cloistered within his chest,
Swirling
Through blue stardust
Snow globe glittering
Currents of air,
He journeyed
Back back
To the gaping mouth
Of the current.
Stepping through
And into
The now
gray masked
extinguished
Unquenched lamenting
Arrested abstraction
Alas,
Cold rock
Shadow cloaking him.

Still in shock,
Beginning in the aftershock

Of this napalm explosive reality
To recalculate,
He ordered his footprints
To track down
The painted wing children.
As well as the wellspring of
cow eyed hoofed claw pawed
Scaled shelled and leathery wrinkled
Offspring.

In waiting.
The earth shaken where wolf
deftly began to rethread
severed roots
of toppled trees.
Anchoring, then raising the giants skyward.
A lightning flash
from his glinting blue eyes,
skies flashed blue.

Martial sensing
The scent
Studying
The map
Of his headstrong paw prints
(Witch could hunt more entirely
minus the weight of his structure form,
climbing up the sides of skies
for a sky eye view.)
He followed the unleashed
steps
bridged
a route
to the ken den
of all kin.
The immortelle where wolf
reached the jagged bad lands
Where the emaiated
tribe had fled.

159

On the cold stones
Their weary broken bodies slept.
He wept a rain of blood
their craving bodies
Absorbed.

"O come to me
You who are weak.
O drink from me
The rich milk
Of dreams."
His tumescent male teats
Multiplied
In rows,
Conjuring the potent
Liquid bone.
One drop of the love milk
To heal
the apocalyptic travesty
tragedy of starved bodies.

And those with beaks, paws
Claws, hands leathery or webbed feet,
But all with tongues
And animal lips
Sucked their sip.

Fostered prospered
Glowing luminous,
The piano ivory keyed
ribs
covered
With plush new flesh.
The lush blue milk
spilled
Over the straw man fields
turned mossy antler fur green.
The antler trees
Sprouted blue leaves

As the elixir
Soaked into the earth
Stimulating birth.

Fractured
Fragile
Eggs,
Sealed healed
whole globes.
The fetal embryos
Pumped up
On yolk
Began  to kick and float

With the nefarious
Trail of apathy
Erased,
Hell was reversed.
The sterile
Flowed
Fertile.

And
The painted wing children
Grew the bone
arched architecture
of wings
Spawning spectrums of feathers

Generating
Uplifting
the flight
Of Leonardo's
Dream seed.

# OLD NEWS

An old friend
she hadn't seen or heard
for three score years or more,
called her
out of the blue
to give her the lame news
with no excuse
told her through the phone's
hearing aid
that she had grown old,
as she had not known
this was hoarfrost gravely so.

A throaty crow
with hot corn cobs for ears,
gripping the telephone wires
anchored to the totem pole,
on wrinkly prong
yellow fever receiver feet,
intercepted the lines
of the electrified conversation,
translating this lipstick
smearing searing
unmuzzled mouth
proclamation.
Shocked, the black bird
fell off the tightrope wire
onto the gravel below,
landing
flat on his nosy beak nose
witch bent
a taddle tail to the south.

Though saddled
with this hot flapjack
just flipped from the frying pan flashing item,

(like a clothes horse
tied up in the clothes line
unable to model the peachy keen clean
clothespin hostage
flapper flapping
slap happy
busty lusty latest fashions)
for the telltale crow
grew hoarse,
groveling before
the little yellow laughing dog ha ha!
that saw it all
laughingstock happen.

2
What with the worried bird's
profile
and ego spent
by having to eat crow
and laughing cow cheese,
he reporter relented repented,
did not write this fat dripping, turning over the spit fact
by plucking Ouch!
another clever novel feather
from his salted tail.
Gripping the pinion
between gnarly wrinkled
educated toes,
writing skulker opinionated skullduggery,
in the universal avian hieroglyphic tongue
singing singeing
hyperbole in the dirt
for the hungry flocks that congregation straight from church flock
to read
the latest smirking dirt (presented signed by the grapevine master)
with their sharp bird's eye view.
No, indeedy,
this greedy Salem salesman
of the taboo tabloids

did not say Boo!
Even though his cobs
were scorched to stumps
with the juicy juicy
newsy news
he forked feet receiver received.

Well all's well
that what was delivered
though savory,
was not slavery
sold down the river

I mean here she was
callously
affronted confronted
out of nowhere,
wearing no wire mesh
helmet or armor,
armed with no saber
to save herself;
with the Grimm brothers
proof less truth,
that she was
a falling star,
a toady voice
blind as a bat
six fingered
wrinkled as a far reaching
now stumped
dried up
old witch
tree.

But there was a hitch,
a flower hatted horse
munching a golden hay day
to barn lean against;
witch's are shape shifters

and a wrinkly Lady of the Lake
turns mirror smooth
with drifting past last reflections.
Too, she felt spanking new
as a blue colt,
not used up
but absolutely
bolting in surprise
at the first frozen flakes of snow.

3
And wouldn't you know
like all of us
she was conceived in sin,
yet by far the curse worse
for it was on the Sabbath Day
the under cover Scarlet Letter cardinal act was performed.
Born in a scratchy "Ah! There's the rub,"
horse hair shirt,
complete with a baby crown of briar thorns
for her Nobadaddy
punishing sentence
creeping repent.

In a mandrake
ginger
feat
of rebellious independence,
she altered
this bleeding indoctrination
of pain
to her own testament,
religiously
wearing horse eye blinders
to steer herself from
her former
horse hair training shirt.
Un binded
from the crucial crux

of the cruxi-
fiction,
shorn of the malignant whipping boy
penalties,
naked
through her 3$^{rd}$ eye
indigo
could see
the raw footage
of the beginning of time;
the rose thorned white fanged Dawn
clawing back You
werewolf black night,
who Alpha stalwart rules
staring swarthy fur country
of fiery condor eyes.

Dawn now reclaiming
naming
her rightful Demeter reign
of crowing pups
growing as they patter their spectrum sky sowing paws,
carrying bones of light
in glowing milk teeth mouths,
blotting out the steely grim forest of night.
This baptismal purification
exorcism exercised
by the sublime Goddess Beast
wolf Mother
Priestess.

4
And finally,
she had allowed
a hallowed
Halloween
magic red haired
dream puff child (that she never lost but saved)
at the cost

of her
the child,
giggling
upside down
rooted in her living room
womb
like a tabernacle candle
that did not bow out
in the drafty rain soaked cave,
poking her in the ribs,
fisty cuffs shredding bad memories
(she kept in her back drawers)
into Kodachrome tinsel confetti,
tossing it like streaming firecrackers
dripping over amusement parks,
tickling her insides
as the shimmering pieces drifted upward
mixing up the pretense
of tenses.
So how could she ever wear
the seriously skin tight
mold of the death mask?
Not now
not ever!

5
Besides
the fire engine
red
haired siren,
cherry bomb zing!
smoking child
in her cowboy silver spurred
bucking bronco boots,
spurred her onward
to let go
let it flow
and double
the most of the journey!

Post Script
As for the private eye
operator bugging
private calls,
gossip monger
stump eared crow—
Why even today
she ate crow
with the crow,
a key lime pie
when she peeked behind the curtain to see
the bird
retired fired laid off
from the tattle tail
nosy bent beak job,
had taken to a cherry tricycle
happy tail feather seated
on cushy foam seat
gleaming chrome bars
pedaling like a mad child
with its leathery crone, yellow legs
smart toes
ringing the bell
Ding! Ding! Ring! Ring!
The local scuttle bug
of the street
scurrying
on its hundred booted feet
away
from the former eaves dropping bird dropping
slinging mud pie mag pie
squealer,
squealing
the mighty trikes'
burning rubber flaming wheelie racing tires.

# THE VOYAGER

Am I you,
are you me?
Ponders
the boy
who
is
both living
and dead,
having made
a Houdini caped escape
from the closing coffin
of a dead star;

during a past to future
Einstein whizzing ear
transition
leafing misty silvery sylvan
century
of horse powered
below the torso,
above-the-ring-around–a-posy
wreathed waist,
the feathered arrow strung
expertly bull's eye target marked
by sinewy armed,
human headed, horse eared
centaurs,
on this tangerine tangible
pulsing green center,
abound with
golden bow lipped
quizzing
women breasted
sphinx.

The reflecting voyager,
connected to his counter
clockwise
terrestrial twin,
as they both made a debut
on this swirling blue
rabbit clouded planet,
by the unbreakable
cosmic genesis thread.
He, to the fuzzy yellowy ducky downy crowned girl
after she blindly pushed,squeezing down the vortex slide
emerging on the other side;
yet now, with wide open indigo eyes
and color spectrum vision;
jinxing death
with her
breech
feet first
feat.
She, yo yo strung
to the enigmatic boy,
he to the rubbery skull wrinkled pink neonate,
as he opened the door to the daylight
Hello hello—
stepped out
on soled ivory keyed piano feet,
into this nectar ambrosial humming bird humming time,
bee tubular sipping palace
amongst the thick green tickling rush lush.

From the green horn
tender foot
zero hour,
she the wooly lamb,
he  the curly horned ewe
with milk leaking teats,
sheperding herding her
by the invisible thread,
his honeycomb dripping dreams

witch she tasted ate.
Transmitted
from the mystery boy,
who by splitting himself
into halves
or fours,
spitting image
cloning himself
could be
in two or more places
at once.
That slender birch tree boy
whose hands
the little green branches
outspread
met with a rainbow choir of birds – tee tee too tee tee tee,
when he Hansel and Gretel
scattered bread crusts
beneath the moody blue crust of wind.

The star dusted boy
chose for repose
the cold stone belly of a crypt,
with an eagle winged Seraphim
lead foot standing
dead eye
on the roof
of the marble womb room
where he slept like the dead. (i e, If his tomb mate remains
tucked under the moss bed, instead of phantom moaning, roaming with his high beam
head light on,
screaming in the boy's face.)
The butterfly yellow haired girl
and the blue lad,
holding starfish five fingers
when they were apart
but together,
dreamed the same dreams;
tales of

four legged human's with fly swatting tails,
chimera chiming, golden cupid bow lipped
indigo iris eyed
unblinking sphinx.

When he windmill
searched
at a slow gait,
the graveyard
where the forgotten
remembered,
encircled by the pike spiked fence,
behind the heart shape
turn the key
lock
gates
of this breathing cemetery,
she read
through his inimical black pupil eyes
the Books of the Dead
written in stone.

In this weed seized garden
clinging to life,
where the infant
emperor night, wearing his quixotic Quixote
Merlin star cape,
sibyl zodiacal crown,
his star outlined crepuscular hand
giving the quintessential
religiously brush stroked
into habitual ritual,
Holy baby blessing,
while slurping from the nearest
ultra violet dripping nebula,
with his luminous  tongue,
while the man in the wind whistled
from the blue sea horse splashing
spinning planet below.

Home to
this gloaming turquoise encroaching esprit
clutching fleecy black sheep cloud
in tottering electric twilight sleepers,
tamed by the boy unchained from time,
as young
as the star hatched
budding
twilight blanketed baby
of every early
sandman moonstone gecko climbing evening.

As ancient as the tottering
leaning on stick branches,
crepuscular suited
blue top hat
stardust bearded
grandfather night,
who turned heel
bending back,
when the little white bitey dog
of the nearly morning
nipped at his thin dissolving
skin,
his blood leaping
into the yellow yolk of the sun.

Celebrating this parallel
universe
they shared,
the incendiary incipient of green marine to cobalt winged neon neophyte,
and the boy who did not grow
wearing his coat of cold
pebble warbling brooks,
bats
unfurling nightshade wings
wrapped about the corn teeth
yellow day
hidden

mouse pointy ear masks,
and fur eared  pussy willows
twitching tails
listening listening,
to the unraveling glistening
nocturnal stirrings.

Then the spiraling curled boy's
tongueless shadow
stepped away from him
to talk with shades
in the tongue of the dead,
the sound of the ghosts'
shadow's
wind in the hollow
moon hook in the nook
voices
bouncing back
as hosts to the shadow
conversing in verse.
Those whose clocks
had stopped
drowned in dirt,
rose in a mist
when the  ghostly florid perfume of roses
flirted with these fluttering memories.

Bold gold eyed Sirius
dog sky paddled
after the boy
whose name was Dream,
barking at fat tuxedo cats below
in beaming lantern voice;
arched bridge back bristling cats
under flaring attack
glaring,
seriously mooning back
with stiff straight
fuck you tails,

from the armor harbor of
hundred armed
pointing
color shouting trees.
After this bloodless fight,
the boy's morning shy dog
paddling
all the way to China
to avoid the Tsunami of light.

The boy anchoring port
R. I. P.
beneath the gravity slain
stone footed
eagle winged
tongueless
Angel,
who bravely balanced
the flighty infant night
on her glowing halo.

Deep in Rem unblinking sleep
this canoe drifting oar less boy
puppet strung
to his Siamese twin sister,
who shared her hummingbird darting
needle beak
recording heart
with lazy drifting feathers
fallen and lifted
from ruby combed yellow legged chickens,
spiraling shell
green beast horns
of speckled cows
in the corn,
crowing raven crows
with a pen chance for tail tweaking,
sapphire eyed dusk blue cranes
zen balanced

on one fishing pole leg,
waiting
waiting
for the wriggling silver plated catch.
Day and night
Night and day
zebra striped
N S E W
carousel spinning
weather vanes,
folded lime orange strawberry
paper swans,
eye helmeted crabs
marching across dunes
carrying high tide
giant ocean vibrating fiddles,
and whatever else she could jam cram
store in her Angel Demon beating winged
chest
of drawers.
Minus her,
his chest
host to vanishing graveyard ghosts
might contain only empty drawers.

Either was neither
but both were each other,
East of the red pony sun
that jumped to its unfenced zenith,
and down down under
the riverbed
waking the green lady of the lake
who could ride astride
the flaming water pony.

West of the graveyard
mercury moon
leaking
into beds of the dead

beneath the marine green sky,
their mermaid streaming hair
still growing growing
spilling out through cracks
tendriling through root hooks
yanking restless
kicking corpses
back into their sleepy hollow lairs.


2
Am I you,
are you me,
we who live above
the Village of the Dead,
where wrinkled
bleary eyed crooked trees
shed their starry manes.

No, I have dared not travel
past to future
and back.
Have not stared
Death
in his eyeless eyes,
seen through his cavernous
Golem pool
reflections,
drank in these secrets,
so only you would know.
O my brother
fed the x-ray blast
of a dying star
so you need not eat
and do not grow,
I fade to know,
when will I die?

And defeated by her atomic love
he man in the moon replies;
When your dancing shoes
are nailed to your feet.
When the blazing candle
behind your eyes
shuts out,
snuffed
by Death
galloping
too near you
your tunneling ears,
on the xylophone horse of bones
that the hardhearted wind
beats too hard
so it can  hear the chimes rhyme
Ding! Dong! Ding!

Then I will know
the vulture of woe,
until mercifully
a funneling hurry cane
brews,
uproots the feet
of  the boy
who is
a pale birch tree
snapping mine whistling
neck and spine.

When the cold stone
imprisoned Seraphim's
vigilant
halo blows out,
as she steps out of
her marble heavy
cast,
as a visionary Angel
unchained from gravity

to eagle sweep
beyond the day
caged sky.

When the baby Bodhi
green dimpled twilight
whines
for his missing friend
of young
is old.
When the sapphire jeweled
heron
that waits
on one reed leg,
with crashing splash
spills the quick silver
darting fish
stored in her beak,
that glimmering
fish tail swish
scaling up
the never ending night.

Will I live again?
She sphinx quizzes him.
After you die
leaving this country of shooting stars
icy comets
sizzling
whizzing across
black masked space.
Far beyond
the Gabriel singing horned
feathered
wizard mapped
translators,
windy wing tipped
navigators
pointing south

under a snowy blizzard of stars
While
icy tails
of shooting stars
swiftly melt
evaporate
hurtling too near
the bloodless sun's
fiery tears.

When the spurred cock's
clock
crows fire
singeing
the moon's pallid cheeks,
ashing out its Geisha face.
After a fairy
Titania
slip of a moon
regrows,
until full-
y
emerges
through a hole
in the east

as a grave creeping
silver
horned beast,
stabbed by the last
spike of light,
leaking
its mercury blood
over the silent singing
dreaming graveyard,
Moon of the dead

# TIMELESS TIMES

The timeless times
of sublime
Seraphim
benediction,
rapt attention
to the fleeting;
the pure
genie genius,
peacock
hundred eye
fantail eclipsing
what

lies—

beyond.

Meeting with the complete
truth;
the metaphoric layers,
classical and personal
history
keenly stimulated
in that instant
when we turn from
Medusa blinded stone,
into fluid glass horned
Pan piping
fluted
awakenings.

As even on this dazed
mundane Monday,
when encased in glass and steel,
gazing through windshield

at mass

of aviary angular gray wings,
windy suddenly,
Saint Valentine's
albescent Arcadian dove
sailboat sails
standing out
amongst  the feather herd,
like fire in water.

Inside the vehicle,
hypnotized mesmerized,
holding my hands together
in praise, bowing
to the epiphany
of mellifluous harmony,
Yen balance
manifesto manifested,
encompassed in this Pontifical pilot compass.
Envisioned in snowy hooded head,
tiny bead eyes,
with birds eye
vista visibility
over the Osiris
fern unfurling
blooms day blooms
erupting through the loam,
and spiraling shell horn
unicorns ceremoniously
leaping through oceanic red tide foam.

Ah Yes!
Coastal postal
Pony express message
delivered
in this cherub breasted
pinion prophecy,

Pontifex Maximus
glowing omen of peace;
leaf pinched in beak
token of laurel wreathe.
A Lone Ranger
Crusader
flashing against the limbo gray. Aye!
Love dove
of gold fish splashing Sun,
and silver gloved Moon;
Hi ho!
Rustling Wings
Away!

2
Another nuptial moment
of the lip less glowworm's kiss,
illuminated encounter
of a second
absolute truth,
conveyed
on this same unveiling day.
Wedded to the royal Buddha
UFO glowing Child's dome
golden pear,
pair of reigning gifts.

A blessing against
the schizophrenic split
bruised blue indigo
serpent fanged lightening
striking slashing
tearing open
the sky flood
of bloodless bleeding.
The drinking roots drunk,
little sucking mouths

and peaking Robin's egg turquoise
scattered shell pieces
of broken sky
breaking through the funereal haze.

This breathing revelation
revealed in stop, at corner pet shop
filled with tiny wrinkly leg hopping
platersesque trilling,
whisker footed wheel gyrating
critters.

A radiant dynasty, gold coin serpent fish,
puffing lips breathing in water,
joining us, through Pisces kissed glass
of Aquarius aquarium.
Fated Ra rayed
vascillating
rippling fin,
gold scales
weightless
luminous
Koi fish.

Cold blooded as a bearded dragon,
O Midas touched
painted by the Gold Finger,
James Bond thriller.
So, I ask you, O spinning windmill finned fish,
would you be
a death wish
killer,
in my small lichen kissed pond
that the vigilant statue
Venus
in her half shell
stands over?
Do harm to my
coppery orange gold fish,

funnel lipped
when vacuming up
lichen and anacorise,
be they the taint
of every other goldfish
yet still radiant gifts,
natural natives
of this rock lipped pond,
and my pretty pets.
I could not chance this.

Do I wish to buy you,
O Yes!
See you, golden lamp
trailing through the liquid  mirror.
O smooth flesh fish
nugget of golden star,
swirling alchemy
of liquid gold.

And if you died
as fish often do
not adjusting to the new
environment,
I would find you floating
on your side,
sight extinguished
from your curious eyes,
fan tail dragging
swirling fins stilled,
a woeful ghost fish.
Or if you disappeared
your radical, fire branded presence
seized
hooked by hungry
teeth or beak,
No, I  could not risk
my visionary soul
to be

chained in that once peaceful water,
believing myself
steps towards your death...

O Royal Dynasty gold dragon fish,
a miniature cosmic reflection
of the smiling Buddha child
wearing Sun Red flaming robes,
rides on your back
gliding
breathing with you through water.

www.ingramcontent.com/pod-product-compliance
Lightning Source LLC
Chambersburg PA
CBHW062100090426
42741CB00015B/3290